MARIE STUART

This is the tragic and compelling history of Mary, Queen of Scots, seen through the eyes of the master historical novelist Alexandre Dumas. Dumas's gifts transform the well-known tale into a dramatic, suspense-filled narrative.

We see all the celebrated and terrible events as if for the first time: the murders of Rizzio and Darnley, the Queen's breathtaking escape from captivity at Lochleven, her imprisonment and execution at the hands of England's Elizabeth.

Translations of Mary's own poems and letters (including the possibly forged Casket Letters that helped seal her fate) create an intimate portrait of the woman that history has both condemned as a criminal and lamented as a martyr.

MARIE STUART

Alexandre Dumas

translated by Douglas Munro

Blackie: Glasgow and London

ISBN 0 216 90021 2

Translation copyright © 1975 Douglas Munro

Blackie and Son Limited

Bishopbriggs, Glasgow G64 2NZ
5 Fitzhardinge Street, London W1H 0DL

Filmset by Doyle Photosetting Ltd., Tullamore, Ireland
Printed by Thomson Litho Ltd., East Kilbride, Scotland.

For Isobel

MARIE STUART

Between August and November, 1838, Alexandre Dumas had been travelling along the Rhine with his friend Gérard de Nerval. In those and the preceding months there had been revolving in his mind the writing of a series of works which would ultimately be issued under the collective title of *Celebrated Crimes*, and which were first published in Paris in 1839–1840.

The inclusion of *Marie Stuart* in such a series may well at first seem rather odd to some readers until it is remembered that Dumas's title was intended to include instances in which the subjects were the victims, rather than the perpetrators, of crimes. For instance, Urbain Grandier committed no crime but his case was also included. The case of Mary Stuart may well be different from that of Urbain Grandier but, nevertheless, it has a proper place in the collection.

It should be mentioned, too, that when Dumas undertook to write the *Celebrated Crimes* he was gathering material for his account of the House of Stuart, which covered particularly the period 1437 to 1587. Either the present volume is a skilfully arranged extract from the chronicle of the House of Stuart, or the latter is an expansion of the matter presented in this translation.

Brantôme and other contemporary writers were Dumas's chief authorities for *Marie Stuart*.—D.M.

On the title-page of the original 1842 edition of *Jehanne la Pucelle 1429–1431* by Alexandre Dumas appears an inscription which translated reads: "There are three voices which cry for eternal vengeance against England: Joan of Arc from her funeral pyre; Mary Stuart from her scaffold; and Napoleon from his rock."

The Translator

Chapter I

There are some names when borne by those of royal blood which seem predestined to misfortune. In France the name of Henri is ill-omened. Henri I was poisoned, Henri II was killed in a tournament, Henri III and Henri IV were assassinated, and as for Henri V heaven knows what fate had in reserve for him, for he never came to the throne.

In Scotland, the name of Stuart has had a similar destiny. Robert I, founder of the dynasty, died in a decline at the age of twenty-eight. Robert II, the most fortunate of them all, was forced to pass part of his life in darkness and retirement because of an inflammation of the eyes which kept them constantly suffused with blood. Robert III sank under the sorrow caused by the death of one of his sons and the captivity of the other. James I was stabbed by Graham in the monastery of the black monks at Perth. James II was killed at the siege of Roxburgh through the bursting of a cannon. James III was assassinated by an unknown man in a mill where he had taken refuge after the battle of Sauchieburn. James IV, wounded by two arrows and a blow from a halberd, died surrounded by his nobles on Flodden Field. James V died of grief over the loss of his two sons and of remorse for having had Hamilton executed. James VI, destined to wear the crowns of Scotland and England, was the son of a murdered father and dragged out a melancholy and timorous existence between the scaffolds of his unhappy mother, Mary Stuart, and his son Charles I.

Charles II spent part of his life in exile, and James II died in exile. The Chevalier Saint George, after having been proclaimed King of Scotland under the name of James VII and of England and Wales as James III, was forced to flee without even the dubious glamour of a defeat in battle. Charles Edward, his son, after the affray at Derby and the battle of Culloden, was hunted from mountain to mountain, from rock to rock, from one river's bank to the other, until he escaped half-naked on board a French vessel finally to die in Florence without being recognized as a sovereign by any of the courts of Europe. And, finally, his brother Henry Benedict, the last descendant of the House of Stuart, lived on a pension of three thousand pounds sterling from George III and died in obscurity bequeathing to the House of Hanover those crown jewels which James II took with him when he fled to the continent in 1688—a tardy but full acknowledgement of the legitimacy of the family which had supplanted his own.

Of all this unfortunate house Mary Stuart was the most ill-used plaything of fate. Brantôme, who knew her at one of the saddest periods of her life, said just as she was leaving France for Scotland, "Those who are moved to write of this illustrious Queen of Scotland have two fruitful subjects on which much can be said—her life, and her death."

It was on the 9 August 1561, that Mary, Dowager Queen of France and Queen of Scotland at nineteen years of age, arrived at Calais escorted by her uncles, Cardinal de Guise and Cardinal de Lorraine, the Duc and Duchesse de Guise, the Duc d'Aumale and Monsieur de Nemours. There, waiting to take her to Scotland, were two galleys, one commanded by Monsieur de Mévillon and the other by Capitaine Albize. She stayed six days in Calais, and on the fifteenth of August after sorrowing farewells to her kinsfolk went aboard Monsieur de Mévillon's vessel accompanied by d'Aumale, d'Elbôeuf, Damville, and other noblemen including Brantôme and Chatelard. De Mévillon was told to put to sea at once and he did so using oars, for the wind was insufficient to fill the sails.

Mary was then in the full flower of her beauty. This was

enhanced by the splendour of her mourning-dress—a beauty so marvellous that it charmed all those whom she set out to please, and which was fatal to most. At about this time a *chanson* was written which was admitted even by her rivals to be well within the truth. It was said to have been written by a Monsieur de Maison-Fleur, a court gallant, and ran:

I see her in snow-white robes, in mourning deep and sad to death, pacing to and fro, the true goddess of beauty: in her hand she bears a shaft from Cupid's cruel hoard, and he, who flutters round, has over blindfolded eyes and uncrowned head a widow's veil on which these words are written: "Die, or become my slave".

At the moment of her departure, Mary, in her full mourning-dress of white, seemed more beautiful than ever. Great tears welled from her eyes as she stood at the stern, heartbroken at having to leave, she waved her handkerchief in farewell to those whose hearts were broken at having to remain behind. In half an hour her boat had left the harbour and they were out to sea.

Suddenly Mary heard loud cries astern of the galley. A vessel coming into port under full sail had, through an error of the pilot, struck a rock; a large hole had been ripped in its bottom, it trembled and then began to fill and rapidly sink amid the cries of her crew. Mary stood pale and dumb with horror watching the vessel as it foundered. The crew, as the hull went down, ran up the shrouds and on to the yardarms to prolong their lives by even a few minutes. Finally, hull, masts, yards were all swallowed by the sea; black spots appeared here and there, but only for an instant—one by one they disappeared and the watchers of this tragic scene, when they saw how calm and solitary the ocean was, wondered if it could not have been a vision which had appeared, and then vanished.

"Hélas!" Mary cried out, sinking back and clutching the taffrail, "what a sad omen for so sad a journey." Then she looked back once more at the slowly receding shores of the country she loved so much, and her eyes which horror had dried for a moment filled again with tears. "Adieu, France," she murmured, "adieu, France." For the next five hours, she sat weeping and murmuring those words.

Night started to fall and her grief increased. As objects on shore became indistinguishable in the gathering gloom and she was called below to supper, she rose to her feet saying, "Now, dear France, I leave you forever with jealous night drawing a veil before my eyes. Adieu, then, for the last time, dear France, for I shall never see you again."

When she went below, her companions formed a circle about her, seeking to console and distract her. But her grief overcame her more and more. She could not answer for her voice was choked with sobbing, and she ate little. She ordered a bed to be prepared in the poop, sent for the helmsman, and told him to wake her at dawn if land was still in sight. And here Mary was favoured by good fortune, for the wind died away and when day broke, France was still in sight. The helmsman, not having forgotten the orders he had received, wakened her and, sitting up in bed, she saw again the land she loved. But towards five o'clock the wind freshened, the ship gathered headway, and the last headlands soon disappeared. Then Mary, pale as death, fell back on her bed, crying once more, "Adieu, France, I will never see you again."

In all truth the happiest years of her life were spent in the France she regretted leaving so bitterly. Born during the first religious troubles, by the bedside of her dying father, the shadow which fell upon her cradle darkened her whole life. Her brief stay in France was like a ray of sunshine in that darkness. She was slandered from her very birth, the rumour being spread that she was deformed and could not live; her mother, Marie de Guise, angry at these malicious reports one day undressed the infant princess and showed her naked to the English ambassador who had asked, on behalf of Henry

VIII, for her in marriage to the Prince of Wales who was himself then only five years old.

Crowned at the age of nine months by Cardinal Beaton, Archbishop of St Andrews, Mary was immediately secluded in Stirling Castle by her mother who was fearful of treachery on the part of the English king. Two years later, distrustful of the security offered by that castle, her mother transferred her to an island on the Lake of Monteith where a monastery, the only building on the island, sheltered her and four young girls born in the same year as herself, all of whom bore the same Christian name. They were known as the "Queen's Maries" and were destined to be her companions through good and evil fortune. They were Mary Livingston, Mary Fleming, Mary Seaton, and Mary Beaton.

Mary remained in the monastery until she was taken to Dumbarton Castle on her way to France after the Scottish Parliament had approved of her marriage to the Dauphin, son of Henri II. There she was handed over to Monsieur de Brézé who had come on Henri II's behalf to escort her to France. They sailed in French galleys which were waiting at the mouth of the Clyde and after being hotly pursued by the English fleet, finally arrived at Brest on the 15 August 1548, a year after the death of François I. The party, besides the "Queen's Maries", included three of her many natural brothers. Among them was the Prior of St Andrews, James Stuart, later to renounce his Catholic faith and, under the title of Earl of Murray, Regent of Scotland, to bring misery and death to his sister.

From Brest, Mary was taken to Saint-Germain-en-Laye where Henri II, newly enthroned, welcomed her with great affection and sent her to a convent where the heiresses of the noblest families were educated. There Mary's mind developed rapidly. Born with a woman's heart and a man's intellect, she not only acquired those accomplishments which properly formed part of the education of a future queen, but she also became proficient in those subjects supposedly within the province of learned doctors. When she was fourteen, she delivered a Latin discourse of her own composition in the Louvre before Henri II, Catherine de Médicis, and all the court. In her discourse, she maintained that women should receive a liberal education and that it was as unjust and tyrannical to confine the education of girls to social accomplishments as it would be to deprive flowers of their scent. It can be readily imagined the kind of reception a future queen advancing such a theory was likely to receive at the most literate, yet formal, court in Europe.

Between the works of Rabelais and Marot, whose writings were beginning to lose favour, and those of Ronsard and Montaigne who were then at the zenith of their popularity, Mary became the queen of poetry and would have been quite content to wear no other crown than that which Ronsard, du Bellay, Maison-Fleur and Brantôme daily placed upon her head. But her destiny was preordained. In the middle of a fête, came the fatal tournament at Tournelles when Henri II, struck in the eye by a lance, was killed. Mary Stuart ascended the throne of France and put aside her mourning for Henri's death, only to resume it for the death of her mother.

Mary had been doubly afflicted and her heart overflowed in bitter tears and lamentations. These are the lines of verse which she wrote at that time:

Into my sad and woeful song for loss beyond compare my cruel grief I throw with bitter sighs for my fairest years gone by.

Was ever grief like mine imposed by destiny? Did ever lady in high estate like me have such sweet sadness to make both heart and eye within a coffin lie?

Who in the tender spring and flower of youth have felt great sadness, and have delight in nothing save regret and the wish to please.

All that was sweet and fair to me has now become my pain; the sunny day is now as black as night to me, and all that was once my delight is hidden now from sight.

I have in heart and eye, one face, one image, which shows as mourning on my own sad face, dyed in violet tone that is the lover's own.

Tormented in my pain I go from place to place, but wander as I do my sadness does not go; I find in solitude both what is bad and good.

But where ere I stay, in wood or mead, perhaps at break of day or when twilight comes, my heart sighs on regretting my absent one.

If I raise my gaze towards the skies his gentle eyes I see from through a drifting cloud; or bending over water I see him in a grave.

Or when I rest, sleeping on my couch, again I hear him speak and feel his touch; in work or play always is he close to me.

No other thing I see, however fair displayed, can my heart be a vassal made: not having that perfection of he who my affection held.

My verse is ended here—this sad lament, its refrain reveals pure love of true intent which separation will never render less.

"It was then," Brantôme wrote, "that she was very beautiful to look upon, for the pure whiteness of her face contended for supremacy with the whiteness of her veil. But the veil being the work of man was forced to yield the palm to the snowy pallor of her cheeks." And he added, "I never saw her otherwise than very pale from the first day of her widowhood for as long as I had the honour of forming one of her suite in France and then in Scotland whither, after eighteen months, to her very great regret, she was obliged to go to pacify that kingdom of hers which was torn by religious strife. Hélas! She had neither the inclination nor the desire to go thither, and I have often heard her say that she dreaded the journey like death itself, for she would have preferred a hundred times to remain in France as simple Dowager Queen content with Touraine and Poitou for her dowry than to reign in her own savage country. But, Messieurs her uncles, some of them but not all, advised her to go and even urged her to do so and afterwards bitterly repented their action.''

Chapter 2

So Mary obeyed her advisers and the very voyage to Scotland began so sadly that when she lost sight of France she felt that she would die. It was then that she wrote the well-known lines:

Farewell, delightful land of France, my motherland the most beloved, and nurse of my early years! Farewell, France! Farewell, my happy days, the ship that separates our loves has borne away but half of me: and part is left thee and is thine; I confide it to thy tenderness that thou may hold in mind that other part of me.

That part of herself which she left in France was the body of the young King who had taken all her happiness with him to his grave.

The one hope left to her was that the sight of an English fleet would compel the two galleys to put about and return. But a fog of quite extraordinary density for the time of year enveloped the Channel throughout the day—it was so thick that the mast could not be seen from the stern-sheets. Under its cover, the little ships escaped the English. It lasted all Sunday (they had weighed anchor on the Saturday) and did not clear until eight o'clock on Monday morning. The galleys, which had navigated at random for all these hours, found themselves in such a wilderness of reefs that if the fog had lasted much longer, one or both of them would almost certainly have struck and gone down as had the vessel they had seen when leaving Calais.

When the fog did finally clear, the pilot recognized the Scottish coast. Under his care the galleys were guided through the reefs with great skill to land at Leith. There, no preparations had been made to receive the Queen. However, she had no sooner stepped ashore than the dignitaries of the town learned of her arrival and came to offer their congratulations. A few wretched horses, whose harnesses were falling to pieces, were collected to take the Queen to Edinburgh. When Mary saw them her tears flowed again, for she remembered the lovely palfreys and carriages of the cavaliers and ladies of her suite in France. In one moment Scotland was revealed to her in all its poverty. The next day she was to obtain a glimpse of it in all its ferocity.

After spending the night at Holyroodhouse, "where," wrote Brantôme, "five or six hundred of Edinburgh's rogues kept her awake with an ear-splitting serenade on violins and rebecks, she expressed the wish to hear mass." But unfortunately, the majority of the city's population belonged to the Reformed religion and were furious that the Queen should begin her reign with this proof of loyalty to Catholicism. They forced their way into the church armed with knives, stones, and sticks with the intention of murdering the unfortunate priest who was her chaplain. He left the altar and ran to her for protection. Mary's brother, the Prior of St Andrews, at that time more a soldier than a priest, seized a sword and placed himself between Mary and the mob. He swore that he would kill with his own hand the first man who advanced another step. His firmness, together with the dignity and dauntlessness of the Queen, cooled the ardour of the converts to Reformism.

Mary had arrived in Scotland in the middle of the fever-heat of the first religious disturbances. A zealous Catholic, like all her mother's family, her presence in Scotland aroused the greatest anxiety among the Protestants. The rumour had spread that instead of landing at Leith as the fog had forced her to do, her intention had been to come ashore at Aberdeen where she would have found the Earl of Huntly awaiting her. Huntly was not only one of the peers who had remained faithful to the Catholic religion but he was also, next to the Hamiltons, the most powerful ally of the House of Stuart. It was said that Mary would have then marched upon Edinburgh supported by Huntly and twenty thousand soldiers from the Highlands and re-established Catholicism throughout Scotland. Events soon proved the falsity of that report.

The Queen was devoted to the prior of St Andrews, son of James V and a noble lady of the house of Mar. This lady had been very beautiful in her youth and despite James' well-known liaison with her, and the child which resulted, she had nonetheless married Lord Douglas of Lochleven by whom she had two other sons, the elder named William and the younger George, who were thus the Prior's half-brothers. Mary was scarcely seated on the throne of Scotland when she bestowed upon the Prior of St Andrews the title of Earl of Mar which was, of course, that of his maternal ancestors; and as the Earldom of Murray had been extinct since the death of the famous Thomas Randolph, Mary in her sisterly affection for James Stuart soon added that title to the one already bestowed upon him.

But here matters became more complicated. The new Earl of Mar and Murray was not the man to be content with the title without the estates attached to it. These estates which had reverted to the Crown when the male lines of the former earls became extinct had been appropriated, little by little, by powerful neighbours among whom was the celebrated Earl of Huntly. The result was that, as the Queen thought it probable that her commands would meet opposition, she put herself at the head of a small army commanded by the Earl of Mar and marched north under the pretext of visiting that part of her kingdom.

The Earl of Huntly was not deceived by the apparent reason for this expedition; his son, John Gordon, had just been sentenced to a term of imprisonment for some trivial abuse of authority which he had committed. Huntly adopted, however, an attitude of submission to the Queen. He sent messengers to meet her and to invite her to break her journey at his castle, and followed the messengers in person to renew the invitation himself. Unfortunately, at the moment he met the Queen, the Governor of Inverness, who was a retainer of his, had refused Mary admittance to Inverness Castle despite the fact that it was a "royal" castle. Murray, convinced that it was useless to temporize with such rebellious subjects, had already ordered the Governor's execution on the charge of high treason.

This fresh display of strength convinced Huntly that the young Queen did not intend allowing her great nobles to resume the exercise of the almost sovereign rights which her father had stopped. For that reason, despite the kindly reception Mary had given him, when he learned that his son had escaped from prison and put himself at the head of his own retainers, Huntly feared that he would be suspected of being privy to this, as he no doubt was. So that same night he left the Queen's camp secretly to assume command of his troops, determined, since Mary had no more than seven or eight thousand men with her, to risk a battle. He claimed, however, as Buccleuch had done before him when he tried to wrest James V from the hands of the Douglas, that he did not war against the Queen, but against the Regent who influenced her unduly and frustrated all her good intentions.

Murray, knowing only too well that the peacefulness of a reign depended greatly on the firmness displayed at its inception, immediately called upon all those northern barons whose lands were near his own to take the field against Huntly. They all responded to his summons, for the Gordons were so powerful already that the fear was widespread of their becoming more so. It was clear that although the lesser nobles hated Huntly, there was no great affection for the Queen. Most of them came without any settled purpose and to let circumstances control their future action.

The two armies met near Aberdeen. Murray at once stationed the troops he had brought from Edinburgh, and upon whose loyalty he could depend, on the summit of a hill, and disposed all his northern allies in echelon formation on its slopes. Huntly advanced resolutely upon his Highland neighbours who, after a brief resistance, fell back in disorder. His men at once threw away their lances and with drawn claymores pursued the fleeing men crying: "Gordon! Gordon!" They thought the fight was already won when suddenly they found themselves confronted by Murray's main body, who stood rock-steady. Their long lances played havoc with their adversaries armed only with claymores. And so the Gordons had to fall back in their turn, whereupon the northern clans rallied and reinforced the Queen's troops, each man having a spray of heather on his bonnet as a mark of identification. This unexpected movement was decisive. The Highlanders swept down the hill in a resistless torrent carrying everything before them. Murray, seeing that the moment had come to change the defeat into a rout, charged with all his horsemen. Huntly, who was stout and clad in heavy armour, fell and was trampled to death. John Gordon was captured and beheaded at Aberdeen three days later; his brother, being too young to undergo similar punishment, was cast into a dungeon and executed when he reached the age of sixteen.

Mary was present throughout the battle. Her calmness and courageous demeanour made a deep impression on those who fought for her. She was heard to say repeatedly that she wished she were a man so that she could pass her days in the saddle, her nights under a tent, to wear a coat of mail and a helmet, with a shield on her arm and a broadsword at her side.

She re-entered Edinburgh amid general enthusiasm for her expedition against Huntly, who was a Catholic but who had once been popular with the people of that city who did not understand the real motives behind the battle. They were of the Reformed church and he was a papist—they had not gone further into the subject than that. In their enthusiasm these

Scots expressed, both orally and in written petitions, their earnest wish that the Queen who had had no children by François II, should marry again. Mary consented and, in accordance with the advice of those who surrounded her, resolved to consult Elizabeth upon the subject of her re-marriage for, being Henry VII's grand-daughter, she was next in succession to the throne of England if Elizabeth died without issue. Unfortunately she had not always been so circumspect, for on the death of Mary Tudor she had laid claim to the throne on the grounds of the alleged illegitimacy of Elizabeth. She and the Dauphin had assumed the titles of King and Queen of Scotland, England and Ireland, had had coins struck bearing those new titles and had had also the armorial bearings of those countries engraved on their plate.

Elizabeth was only nine years older than Mary, being just under thirty. Thus the two were rivals, not as queens alone but as women. In so far as education was concerned Elizabeth had the advantage; she was politically highly-skilled and well-versed in philosophy, history, oratory, poetry and music. Besides her native English she spoke and wrote perfect Greek, Latin, French, Italian and Spanish. But if she was Mary's superior in all these things Mary was by far the more beautiful, and vastly more attractive than her rival. It is true that Elizabeth was majestic in her bearing and agree-able to look upon; her eyes were keen and bright and her complexion dazzling, but her hair was fiery red and she had large feet and hands.* On the other hand Mary had beautiful chestnut hair and a noble forehead;** her eyebrows were open to no other reproach than that of being arched so pre-cisely that they seemed to have been traced by pencil; her eyes had a unique brilliance; her nose was the purest Grecian; her mouth was so rosy and smiling that it seemed formed

* Elizabeth presented a pair of her shoes to Oxford University and from their size they could have been made for a man of medium height.
** Many historians have asserted that Mary's hair was black but Brantôme, who, as has been stated, accompanied her to Scotland and must often have seen it, says it was chestnut.

26

only to murmur words of love, as a flower blooms only to emit its scent, and her neck was as white and graceful as a swan's. Added to all this she had hands of alabaster whiteness, the feet of a child, and the figure of a goddess. The result was a perfect whole with which the most critical could find no flaw.

Mary's beauty was her greatest crime—had there been a single blemish in her face or form she would never have died on the scaffold.

To Elizabeth, who had never seen her in person and could thus judge only by a portrait and hearsay, her beauty was a cause of considerable uneasiness and jealousy which she was quite unable to hide, and which were constantly manifested by her questions and comments. One day she was talking informally with James Melville concerning the object of his mission to her court, which was to ask Elizabeth's advice in the choice of a consort for Mary. Elizabeth, whose first impulse was to urge the choice of the Earl of Leicester, led the Scottish emissary into a study where she showed him several portraits with their names written in her own hand. The first to be shown was that of Leicester, and Melville asked her to give him the portrait to take to his mistress. Elizabeth refused and said that it was the only one she had. Melville then smilingly suggested that as she had the origin from which the portrait had been made she could get along without the copy, but nothing would induce her to part with it. She then showed him her portrait of Mary, which she kissed with much affection and expressed to Melville her great longing to see his mistress.

"That is very easy, Madam," he replied, "pretend to remain in your room under the pretext of being ill and leave incognito for Scotland, just as James V went to France when he wished to see Madeleine de Valois whom he later married."

"Alas," Elizabeth replied, "I would very much like to do that but it is not that easy. Tell your Queen, however, that

I love her dearly and that I wish to live in closer friendship than we have done." Then changing to a subject which she had obviously been longing to broach for some time, "Come, Melville, tell me frankly whether my sister is as beautiful as she appears to be."

"She is considered very beautiful," Melville said, "but I cannot give Your Majesty any satisfactory idea of her beauty because I have nothing to compare her with."

"I will give you something. Is she more beautiful than me?"

"Madam," Melville rejoined, "you are the most beautiful woman in England, and Mary Stuart in Scotland."

"But which of us is the taller?" Elizabeth demanded, dissatisfied with the emissary's diplomatic answer.

"My mistress, Madam. I must admit that."

"Then she's too tall," said Elizabeth peevishly, "for I am as tall as any woman ought to be. And what are her favourite amusements?"

"Hunting, Madam, riding, and playing the lute and harpsichord."

"Does she play the last well?"

"Why, yes, Madam, very well for a queen."

The conversation stopped there, but, as Elizabeth was an accomplished musician she gave instructions for Melville to be brought to her apartments when she was at her harpsichord so that he could hear her playing when she would not seem to be performing for his particular benefit. In accordance with her instructions, the emissary was brought the same day to a gallery separated from the Queen's apartments only by a hanging tapestry. Melville was thus able, by raising it, to listen at his leisure. She did not turn until she had finished the piece she was playing with considerable skill. When she saw Melville, she put on a show of anger and even threatened to strike him. But her indignation was calmed by his compliments and finally vanished when he admitted that she played far better than Mary.

But Elizabeth did not stop there. She was so proud of her triumph that she determined that Melville should see her dance. She held back his dispatches for two days that he might be present at a ball which she was giving; these dispatches expressed the wish that Mary should marry Leicester. Such a proposal could not be taken seriously, for Leicester's attainments were mediocre and he was of too humble birth to make a suitable husband for the daughter of so many kings. Indeed, in due course Mary replied that such an alliance could not be regarded as a suitable one for her to enter into.

Meantime there was a curious and tragic incident at Mary's court. Among the noblemen who had followed her to Scotland was, as has been said, a young man named Chatelard. Through his mother he was a nephew of Chevalier Bayard, and he was a talented poet. He was a member of Maréchal Damville's household and by virtue of that position had paid court to Mary during the whole of her stay in France. She had seen in the homage he had paid her, mostly in verse, nothing more than those declarations of devotion which were then customary and with which she, more than any other woman, was overwhelmed daily.

It happened that fate compelled her to leave France at the moment when Chatelard was most deeply in love with her. Damville, himself encouraged by the reception Mary had given to him and mindful perhaps of succeeding François II in her affections, know nothing of Chatelard's love for her. Without the slightest suspicion that he had a rival, Damville confided in Chatelard, and when he was obliged to be away from her court enjoined the young man to watch over his interests. Chatelard was thus brought still closer to Mary. She treated him, in his capacity as a poet, like a brother. His love for her increased and emboldened him to the point of risking everything to win another title than that of "my poet". So one evening he stole into the Queen's room and hid under her bed. But just as she was beginning to undress, her pet dog began to yap so furiously that her women came running in and quickly discovered Chatelard. Mary forgave him.

But her forgiveness had no other effect than to increase Chatelard's confidence. He attributed the rebuke he received to the presence of her attendants and imagined that if they had not been present her forgiveness would have been even more complete. Three weeks later, the same scene was re-enacted. This time Chatelard was detected hiding in a cupboard when the Queen was in bed, and was handed over to the guards.

The time was ill-chosen. Such a scandal occurring as Mary was on the point of remarrying would have been fatal to her—unless it was made fatal for Chatelard. Murray took the matter in hand and, considering that only a public trial could save his sister's reputation, he pushed the accusation of *lèse-majesté* so vigorously that Chatelard was convicted and condemned to death. Mary made a feeble attempt to induce her brother to have him sent back to France, but Murray convinced her of the terrible consequences which might result from such an exercise of pardon. Mary was forced to let justice take its course and Chatelard's fate was sealed.

On mounting the scaffold, which had been erected in front of the Queen's palace, Chatelard, who had declined the services of a priest, asked that Ronsard's "Ode to Death" should be read to him. He listened with obvious pleasure. When the reading was ended he turned towards the Queen's windows and cried out, "Adieu, most lovely and cruel of princesses!" He then offered his neck to the executioner with neither repentance nor complaint. His death seared the Queen more deeply because she dared not openly show or express her compassion.

Chapter 3

Meanwhile the news had spread abroad that the Queen of Scotland was considering remarrying. Many aspirants came forward, among them descendants of the most illustrious European royal houses. First, there was the Archduke Charles, third son of the German Emperor; then there was the hereditary Prince of Spain, Don Carlos, subsequently put to death by his father; and the Duc d'Anjou who later became Henri III. But to marry a foreign prince now was to renounce her right to the English throne. Mary refused them all, and sought credit for doing so in the good opinion of Elizabeth. Then she considered the merits of one of the English Queen's relatives, Henry Stuart, Lord Darnley, son of the Earl of Lennox.

Elizabeth could find no plausible objection to the marriage, particularly as Mary had not only chosen an Englishman, and one of Elizabeth's relatives at that. She allowed the Earl of Lennox and his son to visit the court of Scotland, retaining the right, if affairs should seem to be taking any dangerous turn, to recall them to England. This they could be compelled to do as all their property was south of the border.

Darnley was eighteen. He was handsome, accomplished, elegant, and capable of the clever and amusing talk which Mary had heard in France but not since her return to Scotland. She allowed herself to be blinded by these external qualities and failed to perceive that beneath it Darnley hid profound ignorance, doubtful courage, and a vacillating and brutal temperament. It is true to say that Darnley in his desire to marry Mary did not disdain seeking the patronage of a man whose influence was as remarkable as his elevation to the position which made it possible for him to exercise it. This man was David Rizzio.

Rizzio, who played so prominent a rôle in Mary's life, and whose extraordinary favour with her provided her enemies with such deadly weapons against her without any probable reason, was the son of a musician in Turin burdened with a large family. His father saw that he had musical talent and had educated him accordingly. When he was fifteen he left home and went on foot to Nice where the Duc de Savoie then held court. He there entered the service of the Duc de Moreto. When, some years later, de Moreto was appointed Ambassador to Scotland, Rizzio accompanied him. He was gifted with a fine voice, was a skilful player of the violin and rebeck, and accompanied himself in songs of which he composed both the words and the music. The Ambassador spoke of him to Mary. She expressed the wish to see him. Rizzio, full of self-confidence, saw in this a means of furthering his own fortunes; he lost no time in obeying and sang before her, to her great delight. She then asked de Moreto to give him to her, attaching no more importance to the request than if she had asked for a thoroughbred dog or a well-trained falcon. De Moreto, only too pleased with the opportunity of doing her a favour, agreed.

Rizzio had been only a short time in her service before she became aware that music was not the least of his accomplishments—his learning was varied if not particularly deep; he had a clear, quick mind, a lively imagination, gentleness; at the same time he showed strength of character and self-assurance. He reminded her of the Italians she had seen at the French court. He spoke to her in the language of Marot and Ronsard whose most beautiful poems he knew by heart. Less talent than this would have made him welcome to Mary. In a short time, he became her favourite. When the position of secretary of French official dispatches became opportunely vacant Rizzio was duly appointed to it.

Darnley, determined at all costs to succeed in his courtship, enlisted Rizzio's help. He was quite unaware that he stood in no need of any assistance. Mary had fallen in love with him at first sight. Through fear of some fresh intrigue on Elizabeth's part Mary hurried forward the marriage as much as proprieties would allow. The arrangements for the wedding were made astonishingly quickly and on the 29 July 1565, the wedding took place under the happiest auguries. The people rejoiced along with the nobility, except for a small minority led by Murray. On the eve of the wedding Darnley and the Earl of Lennox received the command to return to London. They did not obey. A week after the ceremony they learned that the Countess of Lennox, the only one of the family who remained in Elizabeth's power, had been arrested and committed to the Tower. Thus, Elizabeth, casting aside dissimulation, yielded to the first violent impulse, always a weakness difficult for her to overcome, and made a public exhibition of her resentment.

She was not the woman, however, to be content with futile revenge. She soon released the Countess and turned her attention to Murray who was the most dissatisfied of all the malcontent noblemen as his personal influence over Mary was utterly destroyed by the marriage. In these circumstances it was not difficult for Elizabeth to persuade him to take up arms against his sister. After an abortive attempt to seize Darnley in person, Murray called upon the Duc de Chatellerault, Glencairn, Argyle and Rothesay to join him. They collected as many of their followers as they were able and rebelled openly against the Queen—this was the first overt demonstration of hostility which was to have later such fatal results for Mary.

For her part, the Queen appealed to her nobles who were quick to respond and rallied to her side. Within a month, she found herself surrounded by the finest army that a Scottish sovereign had ever raised. Darnley was put in command of this magnificent force. Mounted on a superb horse, he wore a suit of gilded armour, and was accompanied by the Queen dressed like an amazon with pistols on her saddle-bow. She was determined to campaign with her husband and not to leave him for a moment. They were both young and good-looking and they rode from Edinburgh amid the enthusiasm of the population and the army.

Murray and his confederates made no attempt to make a stand. The campaign consisted of marches and counter-marches so rapid and complicated that the insurrection became known as the "Run about Raid". Murray and the other rebels retreated to England where Elizabeth, while pretending to blame them for their rashness, nevertheless provided for their needs.

Mary returned to Edinburgh overjoyed with the success of her first campaign, little dreaming that this was the last favour fortune would bestow on her and that her brief period of success had reached its limit. She soon discovered that in marrying Darnley she had not found a gallant and devoted husband but an imperious and brutal master who, having no further reason for dissimulation, showed his true character. His drunkenness and debauchery were the least of his vices and serious trouble soon arose in the royal household.

Darnley, when he married Mary, did not become king, but simply the Queen's Consort. To endow him with author-ity equal to that of a Regent, it was necessary that she bestow upon him what was called the "crown matrimonial" which François II had worn during his brief reign. This, because of his conduct, Mary refused to do. However urgent his de-mands, and in whatever form he disguised them, he was met with an unvarying and persistent refusal. Darnley was astonished at such resolution in a young woman who had loved him well enough to marry him. As he had no idea that she was acting independently, he set out to discover by what secret influential adviser she might be inspired. His suspi-cions fell upon Rizzio.

It is indisputable that whatever may have been the true explanation of Rizzio's influence (and this point has never been decided by the most impartial historians and has always remained obscure), whether he issued his commands as a lover, or gave advice as if he were a head of department of state affairs, as long as he lived his thoughts were always for the greater glory of the Queen. His origin was so humble that he wished to show himself worthy of the height to which he had risen. Above all, it was to Mary to whom he tried to pay by his absolute devotion all that he owed to her. Darnley, then, was not far mistaken in believing that Rizzio, in despair at having done what he did to bring about a marriage which had resulted in such misery, may have advised Mary not to yield one iota of her power to Darnley, who already possessed far more than he deserved in being married to her.

Like all men of weak but violent character, Darnley doubted the existence of firmness and resolution in others unless they were sustained by some outside influence. He thought that by getting rid of Rizzio he could not but help to achieve his ends because Rizzio alone, in his opinion, was the only obstacle in his path. Rizzio was bitterly hated by the nobility because he had raised himself above them on his own merits. It was not difficult for Darnley to organize a conspiracy, and James Douglas of Morton, Chancellor of the Kingdom, agreed to take the lead in it.

This is the second time in this narrative that the name of Douglas has been mentioned, a name to be met with so often in the history of Scotland. The elder branch called the "Black Douglas" was extinct. The name was carried on in the younger branch to whom the title, the "Red Douglas", was applied. It was an ancient, noble and powerful family which—when Robert the Bruce's male line had vanished—contended for the crown with the first of the Stuarts. From then onwards, it had kept close to the throne, sometimes friendly, sometimes hostile, and watching every other great family jealously in case its own power should be overshadowed. The Douglas were especially watchful of the Hamiltons who stood next to them in power, if indeed they were not equal to them. During the reign of James V, that king's hatred for them had not only lost the Douglas all their influence but had also driven them into exile in England. This hatred had come about because they had forcibly seized the young prince and kept him in confinement until he was fifteen, when he succeeded in escaping from Falkland with the help of one of his pages. He reached Stirling, where the governor was devoted to him. As soon as he was safe in Stirling Castle he issued a proclamation that any Douglas who approached within twelve miles would be guilty of high treason. And that was not all. He procured a decree from Parliament which declared that they had forfeited their rights to property and that they were banished from the kingdom. This proscription lasted as long as the King lived and they did not return to Scotland until after his death. The result was that, although they resumed their old position close to the throne and occupied important offices thanks to the influence of Murray, who was a Douglas on his mother's side, they never forgave the daughter for her father's hatred.

Thus it was that James Douglas, although he was Chancellor of the Realm and in that capacity bound to see that the laws were properly effected, placed himself at the head of a conspiracy the object of which was the violation of every law, both divine and human.

Douglas' first idea was to treat Rizzio as the favourite of James III had been treated at the Bridge of Lauder—that is to say to go through a form of trial and then hang him. But such a death did not satisfy Darnley's desire for vengeance, for it was, above all, the Queen he wanted to punish in the person of Rizzio, and he insisted that the murder should be carried out in her presence. Douglas then brought Lord Ruthven into the plot, a lazy and debauched man, devoted to luxury, who promised to give his co-operation to the extent of wearing a cuirass! Having made certain of one powerful accomplice, he then set about finding others.

The conspiracy, however, was not hatched in enough

secrecy to avoid a leakage, and Rizzio received a number of warnings which he disregarded. Sir James Melville, among others, tried in every way to impress upon him the dangerous position which a foreigner enjoying the Queen's absolute confidence occupied at a court so full of jealousy and as uncivilized as that of Scotland. Rizzio heard these warnings and took little heed of them. Melville, feeling that he had done all that his conscience required of him to do, did not press matters further.

Then along came a French priest who was reputed to be a very skilful astrologer. He saw Rizzio and warned him that the stars predicted that his life was in peril and that he must guard against the treachery of a certain bastard. Rizzio replied that from the day when the Queen had first honoured him with her confidence, his life had been dedicated to her service. He added that he had noticed that the Scots were, in general, quick to threaten but slow to act. As for the bastard of whom the priest spoke, and who was undoubtedly the Earl of Murray, he knew better than to come far enough into Scotland for his sword to reach him, for it was long enough to reach from Edinburgh to Dumfries. This was another way of saying that Murray would pass the remainder of his days in exile, for Dumfries was a frontier town.

Meanwhile, the plot continued on its course and Douglas and Ruthven, having chosen their accomplices and made their preparations, sought out Darnley to clinch the bargain. As a price for the bloody service they were to render him, they demanded his promise to obtain a pardon for Murray and the others who were compromised with him in the "Run about Raid". Darnley promised whatever they wished, and a messenger was sent to Murray to advise him of the plot now in preparation and to suggest that he should hold himself in readiness to return to Scotland at short notice. All this having been settled Darnley was made to sign a statement to the effect that he was the instigator and leader.

The assassins included the Earl of Morton, the Earl of Ruthven, George Douglas, the bastard of Angus, Lindsay and Andrew Carew. The rest were soldiers who did not even know what was wanted of them. Darnley reserved the right to fix the time of the murder.

Two days after the completion of all the details, Darnley, having been told that the Queen was alone with Rizzio, wanted to satisfy himself as to how far her favours extended to her secretary. He tried to enter her apartment by a private door, the key to which he always carried with him. He turned the lock to no purpose; the door would not open. He then knocked, calling out his name. But his wife, who held him in utter contempt, left him standing outside, although even if she had been alone with Rizzio, she would have had ample time to send him away. Angered beyond endurance Darnley sent for Morton, Ruthven, Lennox, Lindsay and Douglas. They fixed the second following day for the murder. All the details had been arranged and the parts which each had to play in the bloody tragedy were allotted. But just when they least expected it the door opened and Mary stood on the threshold.

"My lords," she said, "it is quite useless for you to hold these secret meetings. I am fully informed on your plot and with God's help, I will soon counteract it."

Then, before the conspirators could recover from their surprise, she closed the door and disappeared, a fleeting but ominous vision. They were dumbfounded. Morton was the first to find his voice.

"Gentlemen," he exclaimed, "this is a game of life and death. Victory will not come to the cleverest or strongest but to the most prompt. If we don't make an end to this man we shall lose our own lives. We must not wait until the day after tomorrow, but strike him down tonight."

Everyone applauded, even Ruthven who promised his support even though he was still ill after a drunken debauch. The only change made to Morton's proposal was to postpone the murder until next day, for they agreed that at least twenty-four hours were needed to assemble the minor conspirators who numbered about one hundred and fifty.

The next day was 9 March 1566. Mary, who had inherited from her father his hatred of etiquette and love of freedom, had invited six people, including Rizzio, to supper. Darnley was told of this in the morning. He at once informed his fellow conspirators that he would himself let them into the palace between six and seven in the evening. They replied that they would be ready.

The morning was dark and stormy, as the early days of spring can be in Scotland. Towards evening the wind redoubled in fury and snow began to fall. Mary was with Rizzio most of the day. Darnley, stealthily listening at the private door, could hear the sound of musical instruments and the voice of the favourite singing those melodies which have come down to our day, and which the people of Edinburgh still ascribe to him. They were to Mary a reminder of her happy life in France where the performers, who had come in the suite of the Medicis, had made their melodies an echo of Italy. To Darnley they were an insult. Every time he came away from the door his determination to carry out his revenge was strengthened.

At the agreed hour the conspirators, who had received the password during the day, knocked at a door of the palace. They were admitted by Darnley, enveloped in a heavy cloak, who was awaiting them. The soldiers stole into an inner courtyard where they sheltered in sheds to protect themselves from the cold, and prevent themselves from being seen against the snow-covered ground. A brilliantly-lighted window looked out upon this courtyard. This window was in one of the Queen's private rooms, and the soldiers were to break down the door to it if called upon to rush to the assistance of the chief conspirators at a given signal from that window.

Having given his instructions, Darnley led Morton,

39

Ruthven, Lennox, Lindsay, Andrew Carew and Douglas to the room adjoining the one with the lighted window and separated from it only by a tapestry which hung before the door. They could overhear everything and could rush in at a moment's notice. Darnley left them with the strictest instructions to be absolutely quiet and to enter the Queen's room the moment they heard him call out: "A moi, Douglas!" He then went around by way of the secret passage so that the Queen's suspicions might not be roused by his unexpected visit when she saw him enter by the door he customarily used.

Mary was having supper with six guests and, according to de Thon and Melville, Rizzio was sitting on her right, although Camden has stated that he was standing eating at a buffet. The conversation was lively and unconstrained, for everyone was enjoying that sense of well-being felt when seated at a sumptuous table in a warm, bright room with the snow beating on the windows and the wind moaning in the chimney.

Suddenly Mary was aware of the noticeable silence that had followed the cheerful and animated conversation in which her guests had been engaged since sitting down at table. From the direction of their eyes she knew that the cause of their embarrassment was behind her. Turning, she saw Darnley leaning on the back of her easy chair. The Queen shuddered, for although her husband had a smile on his lips, his expression was so malignant as he gazed at Rizzio that it was obvious that something terrible was about to happen. At the same moment Mary heard a heavy, dragging step in the next room. The tapestry was lifted and Ruthven, ghostly pale and dressed in armour the weight of which he could scarcely bear, appeared in the doorway. He drew his sword and stood silently leaning on it. The Queen thought he must be delirious and wandering in his mind.

"What do you want, my lord?" she asked, "and why do you come to my palace armed?"

"Ask your husband, Madam, it is for him to tell you," Ruthven gruffly replied.

"Explain yourself, my lord," Mary demanded, turning to Darnley. "What is the meaning of this visit, this invasion of my privacy?"

"It means, Madam, that that man", and he pointed to Rizzio, "must leave here immediately."

"That man is in my service," said Mary with a contemptuous gesture and rising, "and so he receives no orders except from me."

"A moi, Douglas!" Darnley shouted.

At these words the conspirators, who had been coming closer to Ruthven for some few minutes, fearing from Darnley's well-known weakness of character that he might not have the nerve to call to them and so would have brought them there to no purpose, burst so precipitately into the room that they overturned the supper table. Thereupon Rizzio, seeing that they were seeking his life, threw himself upon his knees behind the Queen and seizing the hem of her dress cried out: "Giustizia! Giustizia!"

True to her character, the Queen showed no fear at this invasion but remained standing in front of Rizzio sheltering him. But she relied too much on the respect for her of these nobles whose forebears had been fighting against their kings for centuries. Andrew Carew pointed a dagger at her breast and threatened to kill her if she persisted in shielding the man they had come to kill. Then Darnley, regardless of the fact that the Queen was pregnant, grabbed her around the waist and dragged her away from Rizzio who remained white and trembling on his knees. The bastard Douglas, fulfilling the priest's prophecy, seized Darnley's dagger and buried it in Rizzio's chest, inflicting a severe but not mortal wound. Morton took Rizzio by his feet and dragged him out of the room, leaving the long bloodstain which remained on the floor for many years. Then they all fell upon him.

When they were tired of stabbing him there were fifty-six wounds in his body.

While this was happening Darnley held the Queen who, thinking that all was still not lost, did not stop crying for mercy for Rizzio. But once again Ruthven appeared, looking more ghastly than before, and nodded affirmatively to Darnley's question as to whether he was dead. Ruthven, unable to bear any more fatigue, sat down even though the Queen, whom Darnley had now released, was still standing. This was too much for Mary.

"My lord," she cried, "who gave you permission to sit in my presence? What do you mean by such insolence?"

"Madam," Ruthven replied, "it is not insolence but physical weakness which has made me sit, for in order to do your husband a service I have taken more exercise than my doctors allow me." Then he turned to a servant. "Bring me a glass of wine." And showing his bloody dagger to Darnley: "Here is proof that I have earned it."

The servant obeyed and Ruthven drank with as much tranquillity as if he had just carried out the most innocent act in the world.

"My lord," said the Queen, taking a step towards him, "it may be that being a woman I shall never find an opportunity to be revenged for what you have done, but," she added, touching her stomach, "but the child I am bearing and for whose life you should have had more respect, even though you respect me so little, will one day make you pay dearly for all these insults."

And then, with a superb threatening gesture, she left the room by the door through which Darnley had come, closing it behind her.

Just then a great noise was heard on the other side of the tapestry. Huntly, Atholl and Bothwell, the last of whom was to play a prominent part in what followed, were having supper together in another part of the palace when they heard shouting and the clash of weapons. They rushed towards the noise and Atholl, who was leading, stumbled over, without knowing whose it was, Rizzio's body lying at the top of a staircase. They supposed, when they saw that a man had been murdered, that there was some plot against the Queen and her husband, and drew their swords to force the door which was guarded by Morton. But as soon as Darnley understood the reason for their unexpected appearance he hurried forward, followed by Ruthven, and showed himself to the newcomers.

"My lords," he said, "the Queen's person and my own are in no danger, and nothing has been done except under our orders. Withdraw, and you will be fully informed when the time comes."

He lifted Rizzio's head by the hair while Douglas held a torch to the face so that it might be recognized.

"You see who this is, and is it worth your while making trouble for yourselves on his account?"

As soon as Huntly, Atholl and Bothwell recognized Rizzio they sheathed their swords, saluted Darnley, and went away.

Mary had left the room with no other thought than vengeance. But she realized that she could not avenge herself on her husband and his accomplices at one and the same time. So she used all the fascination of her wit and beauty to break Darnley away from his confederates. This was not difficult, for when the brutal anger which often carried Darnley beyond reason had had time to cool down, he was himself horrified at the crime he had committed.

While the other assassins in conclave with Murray were deciding that he should have the crown he was so ambitious to wear, Darnley himself, as unstable as he was violent, as cowardly as he was cruel, was negotiating an agreement with Mary in the room where the blood was scarcely dry—one in which he engaged to betray his accomplices.

Chapter 4

Three days later, the murderers were astounded to learn that Darnley and Mary, accompanied by Lord Seaton, had left Holyroodhouse. After three more days had passed, a proclamation was issued. This was signed by Mary at Dunbar, summoning in her own name and her husband's all the nobles and barons of Scotland to join them, including those compromised in the "Run about Raid" to whom she granted not only full pardon but the renewal of her confidence. In this way she separated Murray's cause from that of Morton. The other assassins, seeing that there was no safety for them in Scotland, sought refuge in England where any enemy of the Queen, notwithstanding the apparent cordiality between Mary and Elizabeth, could always be sure of a warm welcome. Bothwell, whose impulse had been to prevent the murder, was appointed Lord Warden of the Marches.

Unfortunately for her reputation, Mary, who was always more woman than queen and directly different from Elizabeth who was more queen than woman, no sooner felt herself firmly in power than she had Rizzio's body, which had been unceremoniously buried at the gate of the church nearest to Holyroodhouse, exhumed and reburied among the kings of Scotland. She thus compromised herself even more by the honour given to the dead than by favours bestowed upon the living.

This ill-advised proof of her feelings naturally led to renewed quarrelling between her and Darnley. Their quarrels were the more bitter because their reconciliation on her side at least was only a pretence. Mary felt, with the birth of her child getting nearer and nearer, that she was in a position of strength. Throwing aside all pretences she left Darnley at Dunbar and returned to Edinburgh. On 19 June 1556, three months after Rizzio's murder, she gave birth to the son who was to become James VI.

Mary immediately sent for Sir James Melville, her usual envoy to Elizabeth, instructed him to carry the news to her, and at the same time begged Elizabeth to be the child's godmother. On his arrival in London Melville at once presented himself, but a ball was in progress and he could not see the Queen. He had to content himself with telling Cecil, her minister, and asking him to request his mistress to give him an audience on the following day.

Elizabeth was dancing in a quadrille when Cecil approached her and said in a low tone, "Queen Mary of Scotland has given birth to a son."

At these words Elizabeth turned deathly pale and gazed wildly about her as if she were going to faint. She first supported herself against a chair, but was soon shaking too much to be able to stand. She sat down and, throwing back her head, became absorbed in a reverie. One of the ladies of the court elbowed her way through the circle which had formed around the Queen and anxiously asked her the cause of her sudden indisposition.

"Ah madam," Elizabeth impatiently answered, "do you not know that Mary Stuart has given birth to a son whilst I am but barren stock and will die leaving no children?"

But notwithstanding her tendency to yield to first impulses Elizabeth was too shrewd a politician to compromise herself by further demonstrating her annoyance. The ball continued and the interrupted quadrille was resumed and finished.

Melville had his audience on the following day. Elizabeth received him cordially, assuring him of the great pleasure she felt from the news he had brought her and which, she said, had cured her of an indisposition from which she had been suffering for the past fortnight. Melville replied that his mistress had lost no time in informing her of her own happiness knowing that she had no better friend. But he added that this happiness had nearly cost her her life for the delivery had been a difficult one. He emphasized this fact three times in order to increase the English Queen's aversion towards marriage.

"You need have no fear, Melville," Elizabeth finally replied, "and you need not emphasize the matter so much for I shall never marry. My kingdom is my husband and my subjects are my children. When I die I wish the following words to be engraved on my tomb, 'Here lies Elizabeth, who reigned so many years and who died a virgin'."

Melville took advantage of an opportunity to remind Elizabeth of the desire she had expressed some years earlier to meet Mary. But she replied that not only did affairs of state require her constant presence but also that she was not anxious, after all she had heard of Mary's beauty, to expose herself to a disadvantageous comparison. So she gave her proxy to the Duke of Bedford who went north accompanied by several other noblemen to Stirling Castle where the young prince was baptized with great pomp and christened Charles James.

It was noted that Darnley was not present at the ceremony and his absence seemed to scandalize Elizabeth's representative. But James Hepburn, Earl of Bothwell, was very much in evidence. Bothwell, since the evening when he heard Mary's cries and ran to prevent Rizzio's murder had made great strides in the Queen's favour. Moreover, he had openly espoused her party as opposed to that of Darnley and the Earl of Murray.

Bothwell was a man of thirty-five, the head of the powerful Hepburn family which wielded considerable influence in the east Lothians and Berwickshire. He was of violent and brutal temper, addicted to all forms of dissipation, and capable of any villainy to satisfy the ambition which he made no attempt to conceal. In his youth he had been considered brave, but for many years he had had no serious occasion to display his courage.

If Darnley's authority had been weakened by Rizzio's influence, it was entirely overthrown by Bothwell's. The great nobles, following Bothwell's precedent, no longer stood when Darnley was present, and gradually ceased treating him even as their equal. His suite was reduced, his silver-plate was taken away, and the few officers who remained with him showed him little deference. For her part, the Queen no longer took the slightest pains to conceal her aversion for him, and openly avoided him. She carried this avoidance to such an extent that one day when she had gone with Bothwell to Alway she started back again immediately upon Darnley joining them there. He kept his patience, however, until a fresh imprudence brought about the terrible catastrophe which many had foreseen from the very beginning of her intimacy with Bothwell.

Towards the end of October 1556, the Queen was holding a court of justice at Jedburgh when word was brought that Bothwell had been seriously wounded in the hand while trying to seize a criminal named John Elliot. Mary was about to go to the council chamber, but she at once postponed the sitting until the next day, setting off at once on horseback for the hermitage where Bothwell was lying. Although the distance was about twenty miles and the road ran through forests and swamps and across streams, she travelled the whole journey without dismounting. She stayed closeted with Bothwell for some hours and rode back to Jedburgh with equal speed, arriving there during the night.

Although this caused a scandal, augmented and envenomed as it was by the Queen's enemies who were particularly numerous in the Reformed church, Darnley did not hear of it for nearly two months by which time Bothwell, completely recovered, had returned with the Queen to Edinburgh. Darnley could bear his humiliating position no longer. But as since his betrayal of his accomplices, there was not a single Scottish noble who would deign to draw his sword for him, he resolved to go to his father, the Earl of Lennox, hoping that his influence would rally those malcontents who had increased since Bothwell's rise in favour. With his usual indiscretion, Darnley confided his plan to some of his officers who promptly warned Bothwell.

Bothwell seemingly took little notice of Darnley's intentions, but when Darnley had travelled scarcely a mile from Edinburgh he began to feel violent pains. However, he kept on, but arrived at Glasgow very ill. He at once sent for a celebrated physician, James Abrenets, who found his body covered with pustules and unhesitatingly declared that he had been poisoned. There are those, however, and among them Sir Walter Scott, who have asserted that his trouble was nothing more nor less than smallpox.

However that may be, the Queen, because of her husband's apparently dangerous state, seemed to forget her resentment towards him. She sent her own physician on ahead and, heedless of the risk she ran, went to join Darnley. It is true that if letters written by Mary when she was in Glasgow are authentic she knew the nature of his sickness too well to worry about contagion or infection. These letters are transcribed here and it will be related later how they came to fall into the hands of the confederate nobles, and through them were passed to Elizabeth, who joyfully exclaimed when she received them, "Now, by the grace of God, I at last have her life and honour in my hands!"

The first letter:

When I came away from the place where I left my heart judge what condition I was in—I was like a body without a soul. Throughout supper I spoke to no one and nobody dared come near me for it was evident that it would not have been in their own interests to do so. When I was a league from the town the Earl of Lennox sent one of his gentlemen to pay his respects to me and to apologize for not coming himself. He sent word, also, that he did not dare to appear before me after the reprimand I had given him at Cunningham. This messenger begged me, apparently of his own freewill, to inquire into his master's conduct to see if my suspicions were well-founded. I told him that fear was an incurable disease, that the Earl would not be so nervous if his conscience were clear and that if I had spoken rather harshly to him it was no more than a just retaliation for the letter he had written to me.

Not one person who lives in this town has called upon me which leads me to think that they are all in Lennox's interests, and moreover, I hear that all the townsfolk speak well of him and his son. Darnley sent for Joachim yesterday and asked him why I did not stay beside him, adding that my presence would cure him at once; he also asked what was my purpose in coming here and if it was to effect a reconciliation; whether you were here, whether I had drawn up a list of the members of my suite, whether I had taken Paris and Gilbert for secretaries, and whether I was still determined to dismiss Joseph. I do not know who has kept him so well-informed. There is nothing, not even Sebastien's marriage, which he does not know all about.

I asked him to explain one of his letters in which he complained of the cruelty of certain people. He replied that he was in despair but that my presence gave him so much joy that he thought he would die of it. He reproached me several times because he found me dreaming. I left him to go to supper, and he begged me to return and I did so. He then told me of the history of his illness and said that his only wish was to make a will leaving everything he had to me, adding that I was in some way the cause of his illness because of my coldness to him.

"You ask me," he went on, "who the people are of whom I complain. It is yourself, cruel one, whom I have never been able to appease by my tears and repentance. I know that I have insulted you but not in the manner you reproach me with; I have also insulted some of your subjects but you forgave me that. I am young and you say that I continually relapse into the same faults— but is there not hope that a young man like me, utterly inexperienced, may give the lie to appearances, repent, and correct his faults with time? If you will forgive me but once more I promise never to offend you again. The only favour that I ask is that we live together once more as man and wife, having only one table and one bed. If you are inflexible I shall never rise from this bed. Tell me, I implore you, what you intend to do. God alone knows how I suffer, and all because I think of nothing but you, because I love and adore you, and you alone. If I have sometimes offended you the fault is really yours, for when anyone offends me if I were able to complain to you I should never confide my annoyance to others. But when we are at odds with each other I am forced to lock my sorrows within myself and it drives me mad."

He urged me to remain with him and have a room in his house, but I excused myself. I told him that he needed purging but that it could not conveniently be done in Glasgow. Then he said that he knew I had ordered a litter for him, but that he would rather travel with me. I believe that he thought I intended to imprison him. I replied that I would have him taken to Craigmillar where he would find physicians to attend to him, that I would remain near him and we should be where he could see my son. He replied that he would go wherever I chose to take him provided I should agree to one request—he did not wish that anyone should see him.

He said hundreds of nice things to me which I cannot remember, but which would surprise even you. He would not let me leave but wished me to sit up all night with him. I pretended to believe all he said and to appear sincerely attached to him. Indeed, I have never seen him so insignificant, so humble, and if I had not known how emotional he is and if my heart were not so impervious to every sort of weapon except those with which you have wounded it I believe I might have been moved by his pleading. But do not be alarmed for I would die rather than break the promise I have made you. I entreat you to be equally faithful in your dealings with the perfidious creatures who will do their utmost to estrange you from me. I believe that all these people were cast in the same mould. Darnley is always ready to weep, he humbles himself before everyone, from the highest to the lowest, hoping to gain their interest and pity. His father started bleeding from the nose and mouth today, and you can guess the significance of these symptoms. I have not yet seen him for he is confined to his house. Darnley insists that I shall feed him, otherwise he will eat nothing. But whatever I do you will not be taken in by it any more than I am myself. We are bound, you and I, to two most detestable people;* let us pray that hell will break these bonds and that heaven will forge new ones which nothing can break and make of us the most tender and faithful couple that ever existed. There is my profession of faith in which I wish to die.

Forgive this scrawl; you will be compelled to guess at more than half of it, but I know no remedy; I am compelled to write hurriedly while everyone sleeps. But never fear, I take untold pleasure in my vigil, for I cannot sleep as others do since I cannot sleep as I would wish—in your arms.

I am now going to bed. I will finish my letter tomor-

---

* Mary is referring to Bothwell's wife, daughter of the Earl of Huntly, whom he disowned after Darnley's death in order to marry the Queen.

row. I have so much to tell you and the night is too far advanced. Imagine my suffering. I am writing to you, I am talking to you of myself and yet I must stop.

I cannot refrain, however, from hastily filling the bit of paper I have left. Cursed be the madman who torments me so! But for him I might be talking to you on more agreeable matters. He is not much changed; *and yet he took a great deal of it.* His breath is so fetid that it is nearly killing me, for it is much worse than your cousin's. You can imagine that it is a fresh excuse for my not going near him; on the contrary, I get as far away from him as I possibly can and sit on a chair at the foot of his bed.

Let me see that I have forgotten nothing;

His father's messenger to me on the road;

Darnley's interrogation of Joachim;

The condition of my household;

The people who are with me;

The purpose of my coming;

Joseph;

The interview between him and me;

His wish to be agreeable to me and his repentance;

The interpretation of his letter;

Livingston;

Ah, I have forgotten that. Yesterday, at Madame de Rère's supper-table, Livingston said to me in an undertone that he drank to the health of I knew whom, and begged me to join in the toast. After supper, as I was leaning on his shoulder near the fire, he said to me: "Isn't it true that these visits are very agreeable to those who pay them and to those who receive them? But no matter how delighted they may seem at your coming I defy their pleasure to equal the grief of him you have left alone today and who will never know happiness until he sees you again." I asked him who he was referring to. He replied, pressing my arm: "To one of those who did not accompany you; it's easy enough for you to guess who I mean."

I have worked on the bracelet until two o'clock and have tied to it with two ribbons a little key. It is not as well done as I would have wished, but I had not the time to do it better. At the first opportunity I will make you a better one. Be careful that no one sees you wearing it, for I have worked on it in front of everyone and it will certainly be recognized.

In spite of myself I constantly return to the horrible deed you urge upon me. You force me to dissimulate and, above all, to a treachery which makes me shudder. Believe me, I would rather die than commit such a crime, for the very thought makes my heart bleed. Darnley refuses to follow me unless I promise to sit at the same table and share the same bed with him, as before, and not to leave him so often. If I agree, he will do, he says, whatever I wish and will go to the ends of the world with me; but he has entreated me to postpone my departure for two days. I have pretended to agree to his wishes, but I have told him to say nothing of our reconciliation as it might give umbrage to some of the lords. In short, I can do with him as I please.

Hélas! I have never deceived anyone, but what wouldn't I do to please you? Command, and come what may I will obey. But see if you can devise some secret means of doing it in the guise of a remedy. He is to be purged at Craigmillar and to take the waters there; for some days he will not be going out. So far as I am able to judge he is very uneasy in his mind; however, he has great confidence in what I say but not enough to unbosom himself to me. If you so wish I will tell him everything; I cannot have any pleasure in deceiving anyone who trusts me. But it will be just as you say; do not esteem me any the less for it, for it was you who advised me to do it; my desire for revenge would never have carried me so far. Sometimes he attacks me on a very sensitive spot, and touches me to the quick, when he tells me that his crimes are well-known to him, but that greater ones are committed every day, and that it is useless to try and conceal them because all crimes, great and small, always become known and are common subjects of conversation.

He sometimes adds when speaking of Madame de Rère: "I trust that her accommodation and service are satisfactory!" He assures me that many people thought, as he did himself, that I was not my own mistress—that is, without doubt, because I rejected the conditions he offered me. In fact, he is most uneasy on the subject you know about and he suspects that there are designs upon his life. He is in despair whenever the conversation touches upon you, or Lethington or my brother. It is true, nevertheless, that he speaks neither good nor ill of the absent, but always avoids speaking of them at all. His father is confined to his house and I have not seen him. The Hamiltons are here in great numbers and accompany me everywhere; all *his* friends follow me whenever I go to see him. He has begged me to be present tomorrow when he gets up. My courier will tell you the rest.

Burn my letter; it would be dangerous to keep it. Nor, indeed, would it be worthwhile, for it is full of dark thoughts.

As for you, do not be hurt if I am sad and anxious today when to please you I throw honour, remorse and danger to the winds. Do not take what I say in bad part and do not listen to the malicious stories of your wife's brother; he is a villain and you must not allow him to prejudice you against the most affectionate and faithful mistress who ever lived. Above all, do not allow yourself to be moved by that woman; for her sham grief bears no comparison with the real tears that I shed, and with the suffering which my love and constancy lead me to endure that I may succeed her. It is for that alone that I betray, in spite of myself, all those who may throw obstacles in the way of my love for you. May God have mercy on me and send you all the prosperity which your humble and loving friend wishes you and who eagerly awaits a different recompense from you. It is very late; but I always put aside my pen regretfully when I am writing to you; however I will not finish my letter until I have kissed your hands.

Forgive this bad writing; perhaps I have written it so badly purposely so that you might be forced to read it several times. I have transcribed hastily what I had written as notes and my paper has run out. Always remember a loving friend and write often to her; love me as fondly as I love you and remember
Madame de Rère's words;
The English;
The mother;
The Duke of Argyle;
The Earl of Bothwell;
The house at Edinburgh.

The second letter:
You seem to have forgotten me during our separation, yet you promised me when we parted that you would write to me fully on everything new that happened. The hope of receiving your news had given me almost as much pleasure as your return would have done; you have postponed it longer than you promised. As for me, I continue to play my part even though you do not write to me. I shall take him to Craigmillar on Monday and he will remain there over Wednesday, on which day I shall go to Edinburgh to be bled unless you order differently. He is in better spirits than usual and much better in health. He tells me everything he can think of to

persuade me that he loves me, is attentive to me beyond measure and anticipates my every wish. All of which is so agreeable to me that I never enter his room that the pain in my side does not attack me, his company is so burdensome. If Paris brings me what I have asked him for I shall soon be cured. If you have not returned when I go to the place you know of I beg you to write and tell me what you want me to do; for if you do not manage the affair discreetly I foresee that the whole burden will fall upon me. Consider the matter from every stand-point and mature your plans with prudence. I send you my letter by Beaton who will leave here on the day on which Balfour was to have gone. It only remains for me to beg you to keep me informed of your movements.

Glasgow, Saturday morning.

The third letter:

I remained at the place you know of longer than I should have done had I not wished to draw from him something which the bearer of this will tell you; this is an excellent opportunity for the concealment of our plans. I have promised to take the person you know of to see him tomorrow. You must take care of what remains to be done if you approve of the plan. Hélas! I have violated our covenant for you forbade me to write to you or to send a courier. But really I did not intend to offend you; if you knew by what cruel fears my soul is disturbed you would not be so distrustful and suspicious. But I accept it all in good part for I am sure that it is nothing but love which makes you thus, love which is dearer to me than anything else in the world.

My sentiments and blessings are a sure guarantee of that affection and answer to me for your heart; my confidence is without reserve; but in pity's name explain yourself fully; otherwise I shall fear that my unhappy destiny and the too auspicious influence of the stars upon the destiny of women less affectionate than me have made me supplanted in your affections as Medea was in that of Jason. Not that I mean to compare you with such an unfortunate lover, nor myself to such a monster, although your influence over me is powerful enough to force me to imitate her whenever our love demands it, and whenever I am driven to it to retain your heart which belongs only to me; for I call that mine which I have bought with the tender and faithful love for you which consumes me, a love which is more ardent today than ever before and which will end only with my death, a love in short which makes me scorn the perils and the remorse which are likely to be its sad results. As the price of my sacrifice I ask but one favour and that is that you will remember a place not far from here; I do not demand that you keep your promise tomorrow, but I do desire to see you that I may put an end to your suspicions. I ask only one thing of God: that He will enable you to read my heart, which is less mine than yours, that He will preserve you from all ill, at least during my life; life is dear to me only so far as it gives you pleasure to have me live. Adieu, I am going to bed; let me hear from you tomorrow morning, for I shall be anxious until I do. Like the bird escaped from its cage, or the turtle-dove who has lost her mate, in solitude I should mourn your absence however brief it is. This letter, more fortunate than me, will this evening go where I cannot go if the courier does not find you asleep as I fear he will. I have not dared to write in the presence of Joseph, Sebastien and Joachim, and they did not leave me until just before I began.

As may be seen from these letters, assuming them to be genuine, Mary entertained for Bothwell one of those insensate passions which are always the stronger in proportion to the difficulty in accounting for them. Bothwell was no longer young, nor handsome, and yet for his sake Mary sacrificed a young husband who was considered one of the most handsome men of his time. It seemed almost like witchcraft.

So Darnley, the only obstacle to the union of the lovers had long since been condemned by Bothwell, if not by Mary. As his splendid constitution had triumphed over poison they sought other means of killing him.

The Queen, as she had told Bothwell in her letter, refused to take Darnley with her and returned alone to Edinburgh. Arrived there she gave orders that her husband should be taken by litter, not to Stirling or Holyroodhouse, but to the Abbey of Kirk-o'Field. Darnley remonstrated when told of this decision, but as he had not the power to oppose it, he contented himself with complaining of the loneliness of where he was to live. The Queen simply answered that she could not receive him at the moment, either at Stirling or Holyroodhouse, for fear that her son would contract his disease. And so Darnley had no choice but to resign himself to remaining where he was sent.

The Abbey was in an isolated position and its very location was not calculated to dissolve Darnley's fears. It was situated between two ruined churches and two cemeteries. The nearest house was about a gun-shot away—as this house belonged to the Hamiltons, mortal enemies of Darnley, its proximity was far from reassuring. Further away, towards the north, was a cluster of miserable huts called "The Thieves' Crossroads". Making a tour of the Abbey and its grounds Darnley noticed that two holes, each large enough to allow a man to pass through, had been made in the garden wall. He instructed that these holes, through which marauders might crawl, be stopped up and was promised that masons would be sent. But nothing was done and the holes remained open and unobstructed.

The day after his arrival at Kirk-o'Field Darnley saw a light in the Hamilton's house, which he had supposed to be unoccupied. He asked Alexander Durham, his valet, as to the meaning of this and was told that the Archbishop of

St Andrews had for some unknown reason left his palace in Edinburgh and come to live in the old house the day before. This news only increased Darnley's anxieties, for the Archbishop was one of his most outspoken enemies.

Abandoned by his servants one after the other, Darnley lived on the first floor of a small isolated pavilion with no other attendant than Durham. Darnley was particularly attached to him and as, moreover, he was in constant fear of some attempt on his life, he had Durham bring his bed to his room. During the night of the eighth of February, Darnley woke Durham up and told him that he thought he had heard steps in the room under them. Durham got out of bed, took his sword in one hand and a candle in the other and went down to the ground floor. But although Darnley was quite sure he was not mistaken Durham returned a minute later and said that he had seen nobody. The following morning passed without incident.

The Queen had arranged the marriage of one of her servants, Sebastien, an Auvergnat, whom she had brought with her from France, and of whom she was fond. The wedding was to take place on the ninth of February, but Darnley sent word to Mary reminding her that he had not seen her for two days. So she left the wedding festivities towards six in the evening and paid him a visit, accompanied by the Countess of Argyle and the Countess of Huntly. While she was there, Durham, while making up his bed set fire to the straw mattress, which was destroyed as was part of the hair mattress. While they were still burning he threw them out of the window fearing that some of the other furniture would be set alight. He was thus left without a bed to lie on and asked permission to go to the city to sleep there.

But Darnley had not forgotten the preceding night's alarm. Amazed at the haste with which Durham had thrown all his bedding out of the window, he begged him not to go away and offered to let him have one of his mattresses or to share his own bed with him. But despite this offer Durham insisted, saying that he did not feel well and would be glad of the chance to see a doctor that evening. The Queen interceded for him, promising Darnley that another servant would be sent to pass the night with him. Darnley had no choice but to give in. After making Mary repeat her promise, he gave Durham leave of absence for the night.

At this particular moment, Paris, who is referred to in the letters, entered the room. He was a young Frenchman who had spent some years in Scotland in the service of Bothwell and Seaton and was now in the Queen's service. The Queen rose when she saw him and, on Darnley's entreating her to remain longer, said, "It is really impossible, my lord. I left poor Sebastien's wedding to come and see you, and I must return for I promised to come masked at his ball." Darnley dared not insist and simply reminded her of her promise to send another servant to him—Mary repeated her promise and left with her suite. As for Durham, he left the moment he received permission.

It was nine o'clock. Darnley, left alone, carefully secured all the doors on the inside and went to bed ready to get up and let in the new servant who was to spend the night with him. He had scarcely got into bed when he heard the same noise which had startled him the night before. He listened with the strained intentness of fear, and soon was absolutely certain that several men were moving about below. To call for help was useless and to leave his room dangerous; to wait was the only course left to him. He reassured himself that the doors to his room were securely shut, put his sword under his pillow, extinguished his lamp lest its light might betray him, and waited in silence for the servant to arrive. The hours rolled slowly by and no servant appeared.

At one o'clock in the morning, after a long talk with the Queen in the presence of the captain of the guard, Bothwell returned to his quarters for a change of clothing. A little later he came out wrapped in the long cloak of a German hussar, walked through the guardhouse and had the castle gate opened for him. Once outside he hurried to Kirk-o'Field and entered the grounds through one of the holes in the wall. He had taken only a few steps in the garden when he met James Balfour, governor of Edinburgh Castle.

"Well," he asked, "how are the preparations going?"

"Everything is ready," Balfour replied, "and we were only awaiting your arrival to light the match."

"Good," Bothwell rejoined, "but I must first make sure he is in his room."

He then opened the pavilion door with an extra key, crept up the stairs on tiptoe and listened at Darnley's door. Darnley having heard no further noise had at last dropped off to sleep, but his irregular breathing showed how troubled his sleep was. It was of little importance to Bothwell whether his sleep was troubled or untroubled, so long as he was really in his room. He crept down the stairs as softly as he had come up and, taking a lantern from one of the conspirators, went into the downstairs room to see for himself whether everything was ready. This room was full of casks of gunpowder and a fuse was laid ready which only needed a spark to communicate its flame to the waiting volcano. Bothwell then retreated to the end of the garden with Balfour, David, Chambers, and three or four others, leaving one man to light the fuse. A moment later this man joined them.

Some anxious minutes followed, during which the conspirators silently looked at each other as if afraid of themselves. Then, as there was no explosion, Bothwell turned impatiently to the man who was to have lighted the fuse and reproached him for having failed to do so, doubtless because he was afraid. He assured his master that everything was in order. When Bothwell in his impatience started off to return to the house to make sure he offered to return himself to see what the trouble was. In fact he did go back to the pavilion, looked through a sort of air vent, and saw that the fuse was still burning. He rushed back to Bothwell and the others and was just making signals to them that all was well when there was a terrible explosion. The pavilion seemed to rise bodily in the air, and the city and surrounding countryside were illuminated by a fierce glare which surpassed that of the brightest day. Then all was darkness. The silence was broken only by the noise of falling stones and beams of wood, as thick as hail in a storm.

Darnley's body was found next day in a neighbouring field. It had been protected from the fire by the mattresses upon which he had been lying. He had thrown himself on his bed in dressing-gown and slippers, and was found in the same condition except that the slippers had fallen a few feet from where his body lay. Many people thought that he had been strangled and carried there, but the most probable theory is that the murderers had relied solely on the gunpowder, for it in itself was sufficiently powerful for them to have no fear that it would fail in its purpose.

Chapter 5

Was the Queen, or was she not, an accomplice?

No one has ever known except herself, Bothwell, and God. But, accomplice or not, her conduct, imprudent now as always, gave a semblance of truth if not absolute certainty to the accusations of her enemies. As soon as she was told of the catastrophe, she ordered the corpse to be brought to her. As it lay upon a table she gazed at it for some little time with more curiosity than grief. It was afterwards embalmed, and was buried that same night, without ceremony, beside Rizzio.

Scottish etiquette prescribed that a royal widow should remain for forty days in a darkened room. But on the twelfth day Mary ordered the windows to be thrown open. On the fifteenth, she left with Bothwell for Seaton, a country house some six miles from Edinburgh. Ducroe, the French ambassador, sought her out there and remonstrated with her to such effect that he induced her to return to the capital. But instead of the acclaim which ordinarily greeted her coming, she was received with a freezing silence, broken by one woman in the crowd crying out, "May God treat her as she deserves!"

The identity of the murderers was no secret to the people. Bothwell took a magnificent coat which was too large for him to a tailor, instructing him to alter it to fit him. The man recognized it as having belonged to Darnley.

"That's quite right," Bothwell said, "it is customary for the executioner to inherit his victim's property."

Meantime, the Earl of Lennox, supported by public opinion, clamoured for justice for his son's death and came forward himself as accuser of his murderers. The Queen was forced, in order to appease the paternal anger and the public resentment, to command the Earl of Argyle, the chief of the Scottish judiciary, to inquire into the matter. On the same day the order was given a proclamation was posted in the streets of Edinburgh. It offered in the Queen's name, a reward of two thousand pounds to anyone who would give information concerning her husband's murderers. The following day, printed sheets were stuck next to the official proclamations:

While it has been publicly announced that those who disclose Darnley's assassins should receive two thousand pounds, I, who have made careful enquiries, declare that the criminals are the Earl of Bothwell, James Balfour, the priest of Flitz, David, Chambers, Blackmester, John Spens, and the Queen herself.

These sheets were quickly torn down, but as always happens in such cases they had already been read by most of the population.

The Earl of Lennox accused Bothwell. Public opinion backed him up with such vehemence that Mary was compelled to allow him to be brought to trial, but every precaution was taken to make it impossible for him to be convicted. On the twenty-eighth of March Lennox was advised that the trial was set down for the twelfth April, thus giving him only two weeks to collect incontrovertible evidence against the most powerful man in Scotland. Lennox, realizing the futility of such an attempt and that the trial would be nothing more than a travesty, did not appear. On the other hand, Bothwell was accompanied to the court by five thousand of his supporters as well as two hundred hand-picked fusiliers who mounted guard at the court's doors as soon as he had entered. His attitude was more that of a king preparing to violate the law than an accused person prepared to submit to its judgment. The expected result followed, and the jury acquitted Bothwell of the charge of which everyone, including the judges, knew him to be guilty.

Following the acquittal Bothwell had the following challenge posted in the streets:

Although I am sufficiently exonerated from complicity in this murder of which I have been falsely accused, nevertheless, the better to justify my innocence, I am willing to do battle against anyone who dares assert I am the murderer.

The following reply appeared beside the foregoing on the following day:

I accept the challenge providing that you choose neutral ground.

It was unsigned.

Immediately following on Bothwell's acquittal, rumours spread that the Queen was to marry him. Strange and mad as such a marriage would seem to be, the relations between the two were so well-known that no one doubted the truth of these rumours. But either fear or ambition had brought everyone under Bothwell's subjection. Only two men dared to protest in advance against the union; they were Lord Herries and James Melville.

Mary was at Stirling when Lord Herries, profiting by Bothwell's temporary absence, threw himself at her feet and begged her not to throw her honour away by marrying her husband's murderer, for by doing so those who still doubted would inevitably be convinced that she was his accomplice. But instead of expressing gratitude to Herries for his devotion, the Queen seemed amazed by his audacity and contemptuously told him to rise, saying frigidly that her heart was not Bothwell's and that if she ever remarried she would neither forget what she owed to her people nor what she owed to herself.

Melville did not allow Herries' lack of success to discourage him. He pretended to have received a letter from one of his friends, named Thomas Bishop, written by him in England. He showed this letter to the Queen who, after reading the first few lines, recognized her ambassador's style and his devotion to her, and handed the letter to the Earl of Lethington who was present.

"Here is a very odd letter," she said, "read it. It is a little subterfuge by Melville."

Lethington glanced at the letter, but before he had read half of it, he seized Melville's hand and led him to a window.

"My dear Melville, you were certainly mad just now when you gave this letter to the Queen, for as soon as Bothwell hears about it, and it will not be long, he will have you assassinated. It is true you have acted like an honourable man, but at court it is better to act the part of a clever politician. I would advise you to leave the court as quickly as possible.

Melville did not wait for the advice to be repeated and kept out of sight for a week. Lethington was right. As soon as Bothwell returned to the Queen he knew all that had happened. Furious with Melville, he sought him everywhere, but he could not find him.

These symptoms of opposition, feeble as they were, alarmed Bothwell. Sure of the Queen's affection he determined to hurry things along. So, as the Queen was returning to Edinburgh from Stirling a few days later, Bothwell suddenly appeared at the Bridge of Cramond with a thousand horsemen who were ordered to disarm Huntly, Lethington and Melville, the last having resumed his attendance on the Queen. He seized the Queen's horse by the bridle and with a show of violence compelled her to retrace her steps and accompany him to Dunbar. She did this without the least resistance—an extraordinary thing for her to do, considering her character.

On the following day, the Earls of Huntly and Lethington, and Sir James Melville, as well as their retainers, were freed. Ten days later Mary and Bothwell returned to Edinburgh apparently completely reconciled. On the second day after their return Bothwell gave a dinner at a tavern to his adherents among the nobility. After the meal on the very table at which they had eaten, and amid the half-empty glasses

and overturned bottles, Lindsay, Ruthven, Morton, Maitland, and some ten or twelve other nobles, signed a document
in which they not only swore that Bothwell was innocent but
also recommended him to the Queen as a fitting person to
be her husband. This document ended with the extraordinary
declaration: "After all, the Queen cannot do otherwise
since the Earl has abducted her and slept with her."

However, there were still two obstacles to the marriage.
First, Bothwell had already been married three times and all
three of his former wives were living; secondly, since he had
abducted the Queen, that fact might invalidate any alliance
which she might enter into with him. The first of these
obstacles was dealt with first as being the more difficult to
overcome.

Bothwell's first two wives were of humble birth so he
disdained to worry about them. But it was not so with the
third who was the daughter of that Earl of Huntly who had
been trampled to death by his horse and the sister of the
Gordon who had been beheaded. Happily for Bothwell his
past behaviour made his wife as eager for a divorce as he was
It was thus an easy matter to persuade her to bring a charge of
adultery against her husband. Bothwell admitted that he had
committed adultery with a relative of his wife. The Archbishop of St Andrews, the same who had gone and lodged in
the deserted house at Kirk-o'Field in order to be present at
Darnley's death, pronounced the decree of dissolution. The
suit was entered, tried, and decided within ten days.

As for the second obstacle, relating to the Queen's simul-
ated abduction, Mary undertook to remove that herself.
She went before a tribunal and declared that she not only
forgave Bothwell for his conduct towards her but that she
proposed to heap fresh honours upon him as a loyal and
faithful subject. In effect, a few days later, she created him
Duke of Orkney and on the fifteenth of June, barely four
months after Darnley's death, with a levity bordering on
madness Mary, who had asked for a dispensation to marry a

67

Catholic prince who was a third cousin, married Bothwell who, notwithstanding his divorce, was still a bigamist and now had four wives including the Queen.

The wedding was a gloomy affair as befitted a ceremony performed under such bloody auspices. The only guests were Morton and Maitland and some other of Bothwell's parasites. The French Ambassador, who was a follower of the House of Guise, as was the Queen, refused to attend.

Mary's illusion was short-lived. She was no sooner in Bothwell's power than she realized what sort of a creature she had married. Coarse, brutal, and violent, he seemed to have been chosen by Providence to punish Mary for the sins he had instigated or helped her to commit. His treatment of her became so outrageous that Mary, driven one day beyond endurance, snatched a dagger from Erskine who was present with Melville at one of their scenes, and tried to stab herself—crying out that death was preferable to the life she lived. And yet, incomprehensible as it may seem, in spite of his incessant brutality Mary, forgetting that she was a woman and a queen, was always the first to seek a reconciliation with a child's submissive affection.

Nevertheless these public scenes gave certain nobles the pretext they sought to rise in revolt. The earls of Argyle, Atholl, Glencairn, Lindsay, Boyd, and even Morton and Maitland themselves, Bothwell's never-failing confederates, took up arms with the avowed purpose of avenging Darnley's death and rescuing his son from the hands of the man who had killed his father and was keeping his mother almost in bondage. As for Murray he had kept completely out of the way during all these last events, living in Fife when Darnley was murdered. Three days before Bothwell's so-called trial he had asked and obtained permission from his sister to travel on the continent.

The uprising took place so suddenly that the insurrectionists, whose plan was to seize both Mary and Bothwell by surprise, expected to succeed at the first attempt. The Queen and Bothwell were being entertained by Lord Borthwick and were having a meal when they were told that the house was surrounded by a considerable force of armed men. They had no doubt that it was they who were sought and as they had no means of resistance Bothwell dressed himself in a groom's clothes and Mary in those of a page. Thus clad they rode out of one gate as the confederates entered by another. The two fugitives went to Dunbar.

There they assembled all of Bothwell's friends and made them sign a kind of treaty whereby they promised to defend the Queen and her husband. While this was going on Murray arrived back from France and Bothwell presented the "treaty" to him as well, but Murray refused to sign maintaining that it was an insult to him to suggest that he needed to bind himself in writing to defend his sister and his Queen. His refusal led to an altercation with Bothwell. Murray, true to his doctrine of neutrality, retired to his estates and left the affairs of the realm to follow their fatal course without him.

However, the confederates, having been foiled at Borthwick, did not feel strong enough to attack Bothwell at Dunbar but marched to Edinburgh where they were in contact with a man in whom Bothwell had implicit confidence. He was James Balfour, governor of the Castle, the same man who had superintended the preparation of the explosives which killed Darnley. Bothwell had met him when he entered the garden of Kirk-o'Field. Balfour turned over Edinburgh Castle to the confederates and also handed them a little silver casket engraved with the letter 'F' surmounted by a crown indicating that it had belonged to François II. In fact, it was a gift to the Queen from her first husband which she had passed on to Bothwell.

Balfour asserted that the casket contained valuable papers which in the existing circumstances could be of the greatest use to Mary's enemies. When it was opened, they found copies of the three letters, apparently written by the Queen, the marriage contract between Mary and Bothwell, and twelve pieces of verse in the Queen's handwriting. As Balfour remarked, it was a precious discovery for Mary's enemies and was worth much more than a victory, for the success of their arms would simply put the Queen's life in their hands while Balfour's treachery had betrayed her honour to them.

In the meantime, Bothwell had been levying troops and believed that he was strong enough to fight. Without waiting to be reinforced by the Hamiltons who were assembling their supporters, he moved his army. On 15 June 1567, the opposing forces came face to face. Mary, who wished above all to avoid bloodshed, at once sent the French Ambassador to urge the confederates to lay down their arms. But they replied that the Queen was mistaken in taking them for rebels; that it was not against her, but against Bothwell that they were in arms. The Earl's friends then did all they could to break off negotiations and precipitate a battle—but it was too late. The levied troops had discovered that they were enlisted in the cause of one man only and were expected to fight to gratify a woman's caprice, and not for their country's good. So they boldly announced that since it was Bothwell alone that was aimed at, it was he who must defend his own cause. And he, vain and blustering as ever, proclaimed that he was ready to prove his innocence, sword in hand, against anyone who should maintain that he was guilty.

On the instant, every man of noble birth in the opposing camp accepted the challenge. Eventually all the others gave way to those reputed to be the most valorous—Kirkcaldy of Grange, Murray of Tullibardine, and Lindsay of Byres, each in turn defied him. But whether his courage failed him, or whether at the crucial moment he doubted the justice of his cause, Bothwell sought to evade combat by such amazing pretexts that even the Queen was ashamed and his most devoted friends began to murmur.

Thereupon Mary, perceiving the alarming discontent among their own forces, determined not to risk a battle. She sent a herald to Kirkcaldy of Grange, who was in command of an advanced position. As he came forward to meet the Queen, Bothwell, furious at his own cowardice, ordered a soldier to fire on him; but Mary herself interposed, forbidding under pain of death to the offender any violence. Simultaneously, the report of Bothwell's rash order spread through the army. The mutterings were so threatening that it was clear to him that his cause was altogether lost.

And so, obviously, the Queen thought also for the outcome of her conference with Kirkcaldy was an agreement on her part to abandon Bothwell and to join the confederates on condition that they laid down their arms and escorted her back to Edinburgh as their sovereign. Kirkcaldy returned to his fellow peers with her two conditions and promised to return the following day with a satisfactory reply.

But when the parting from Bothwell was at hand, Mary was seized again with that fatal love for him which she could never overcome. She was so overwhelmed with grief that she wept bitter tears, and announced publicly her intention of sending a message to Kirkcaldy that all negotiations were broken off. Bothwell, however, realizing that his life was no longer safe in his own camp, insisted that matters should be left as they stood. Leaving Mary in tears, he mounted his horse and rode off at full speed, not stopping until he reached Dunbar.

At the appointed hour on the following morning, trumpets announced Kirkcaldy's arrival. Mary immediately mounted and rode out to meet him. As he dismounted to salute her she said,

"My lord, I place myself in your hands on the conditions proposed yesterday, and here is my hand in token of good faith."

Kirkcaldy knelt and respectfully kissed her hand. He then rose and taking her horse by the bridle he led her to the confederate camp. She was received with the utmost respect by the nobility, but not so by the ordinary soldiers. As she passed through the ranks which had been formed there was considerable ominous muttering and several voices called out, "To the stake with the adulteress! To the stake with the murderess!"

Mary stoically endured these insults, but a far worse trial was in store for her. A banner was suddenly unfurled before her eyes. One side depicted Darnley lying dead in the fatal garden, the other showed the young prince on his knees with clasped hands and uplifted eyes with the device, "Oh God! Judge and avenge my cause!"

Seeing this, Mary drew in her horse and started to turn back, but she had taken only a few paces when the accusing banner barred her way. Whichever way she went, she met that hideous ensign. Ceaselessly, for two hours, she had before her eyes Darnley's body calling out for vengeance and the young prince, their son, praying God to punish the assassins. At last she could bear the sight no longer and, with a cry, fell back unconscious upon her saddle and would have fallen to the ground had those close to her not supported her.

That evening, she entered Edinburgh still preceded by that cruel banner, having already more the appearance of a prisoner than a queen. She had not had a moment during the day to attend to her appearance—her hair was dishevelled, her face was ghastly pale and bore the marks of tears. Her clothes were covered with dust and mud. As she rode further and further into the city the hooting and cursing of the crowd followed her. At last, half dead with exhaustion, weighed down with sorrow and bent with shame, she reached the Lord Provost's house. There it seemed as if the whole population of Edinburgh swarmed into the square. Their cries from time to time assumed a terrifying and threatening character. Mary made several attempts to appear at the window hoping that the mere sight of her, which had so often proved irresistible, would disarm the howling crowd. But each time she approached her eyes fell upon that ghastly banner waving between her and the people like a bloodstained curtain, an appalling interpreter of the feelings of the mob.

And yet, all this hatred was directed against Bothwell rather than against the Queen. In Darnley's widow they were hunting Bothwell. The curses were aimed at him; he was the adulterer and he was the coward, while Mary was the weak, infatuated woman who gave fresh proof of her infatuation that night.

As soon as darkness had made the crowd disperse, and the quietness was to some extent restored, Mary's thoughts, being no longer absorbed in her own danger, turned again to Bothwell whom she had been compelled to abandon. At that moment, he was a fugitive and an outlaw whereas she, as she supposed, was about to resume the title and authority of Queen. With a woman's eternal confidence in the power of her own love, with which she always measures the love of another, she believed that Bothwell's greatest regret was not the loss of wealth and power, but of herself. She therefore wrote him a long letter in which, forgetting herself entirely, she promised with words of the most tender affection that she would never abandon him, but would summon him to her side immediately the confederate nobles should become divided and make it possible for her to do so. Having finished the letter, she called a soldier and giving him a purse full of gold ordered him to take the letter to Dunbar, where Bothwell should be. But if he was no longer there, to follow him until he overtook him.

Then she went to bed and slept peacefully, for, unhappy as she was, she believed she had mitigated suffering greater than her own.

Mary was awakened next morning by the tread of an armed man in her room.

Amazed and alarmed at this breach of etiquette, which boded fresh trouble, she sat up. Drawing the hangings, she saw Lindsay of Byres standing before her. He was, as she knew, one of her oldest and bitterest enemies. In a voice which she strove vainly to keep steady, she asked him what he wanted with her at such an hour.

"Do you recognize this writing, Madam?" Lindsay demanded brusquely as he handed the Queen the letter she had written to Bothwell during the night, which the soldier had passed to the confederate nobles instead of setting out with it to Bothwell.

"Yes, indeed, my lord," the Queen replied, "but am I then a prisoner whose correspondence is intercepted, or is it no longer permissible for a wife to write to her husband?"

"When the husband is a traitor, Madam, it is not permissible for a wife to write to him unless she sympathizes with his treason. This seems to be proven by your promise to recall the scoundrel."

"My lord," Mary cried, "you forget that you are speaking to your Queen."

"There was a time, Madam," Lindsay retorted, "when I would have addressed you more humbly and with my knee on the ground, although it is against our old Scottish nature to model ourselves on French courtiers. But for some time past, thanks to your fickle love affairs, you have kept us so much in the field with our armour on our backs that our voices have grown roughened by the cold night air and our stiffened knees refuse to bend. You must, therefore, accept me as I am, Madam, now that for Scotland's happiness you are no longer free to choose your favourites."

Mary turned pale at this lack of respect to which she was so unaccustomed, but restrained her anger as much as she could.

"And yet, my lord," she said, "however well disposed I may be to accept you as you are, I must at least know in what capacity you intrude upon me. This letter which you are holding would indicate that you are a spy. But your readiness to enter my room without being announced leads me to think that you are my gaoler. Pray be kind enough, therefore, to tell me by which of these two names I should call you."

"By neither, Madam, for I am nothing more than your

travelling companion, the commander of the escort to take you to Lochleven Castle, your future residence. Once there, I shall be obliged to leave you and to return here and assist the confederate nobles to choose a Regent for the kingdom."

"And so it was as a prisoner not as Queen that I placed myself in the hands of Kirkcaldy. If I remember aright, such was not our agreement, but I am glad to learn how little time it needs for Scottish nobles to be false to their oaths."

"Your Majesty forgets that these engagements were conditional."

"Upon what?"

"On your promise to separate forever from the murderer of your husband. And here is the proof," he added, pointing to the letter, "that you forgot your promise before we ever thought of breaking faith."

"For what hour is my departure fixed?" Mary asked, beginning to weary of the discussion.

"Eleven o'clock, Madam."

"Very well, my lord, and as I should not like to keep your lordship waiting, you will have the goodness as you withdraw to send someone to help me dress, unless I am reduced to waiting on myself."

As she finished speaking Mary made such an imperious gesture that Lindsay bowed and went out without speaking, however inclined he may have been to retort. A moment later Mary Seaton entered the room.

Chapter 6

The Queen was ready at the appointed time. Such had been her suffering in Edinburgh that she left it without the least regret. Whether to spare her a repetition of the humiliation of the previous day, or to conceal her departure from those who might still be considered her supporters, a litter had been prepared for her. Mary entered this without a word of remonstrance and after a journey of two hours arrived at Duddingston. A small boat was waiting there which set sail as soon as she was on board. The next morning at daybreak she landed in Fife. A stop was made at Rosyth Castle for breakfast, after which they took to the road again, for Lindsay announced that he was anxious for them to reach their destination by nightfall. Just as the sun was sinking, Mary saw the high towers of Lochleven Castle on a small island in the loch.

The royal prisoner was undoubtedly expected, for as soon as the escort reached the loch's shores, Lindsay's page unfurled his banner and waved it. At the same time, his master blew a blast on a small hunting-horn which he wore at his side. Immediately a boat with four sturdy rowers put off from the island and came towards the party. Mary stepped on board without speaking and sat at the stern, while Lindsay and his page sat in front of her. As her guardian seemed no more disposed for conversation than herself, she had abundant time to examine her future place of residence.

The castle, or rather the fortress, of Lochleven, from its position and the character of its architecture, was sombre and gloomy enough under the most favourable of circumstances. But the hour at which Mary's eyes first fell upon it made its general effect even more depressing. As far as could be judged, through the mists rising from the loch, it was one of those massive structures of the twelfth century which are so firmly closed to light and air that they seem like the stone armour of giants. As she drew nearer Mary could distinguish the outlines of two great round towers standing at opposite corners which gave to the building the forbidding aspect of a state prison. A clump of old trees against the northern face, shut in by a high wall resembling a rampart, and seeming to be growing out of the living rock, completed the dismal picture.

However if she looked away from the castle to the west or north, the view, ranging from isle to isle, stretched away across Kinross. Towards the south, it was bounded by the serrated peaks of the Lomonds, their foothills sloping down to the shore of the loch.

Three people were awaiting Mary at the gate of the castle. They were Lady Douglas, her son William Douglas, and a child of twelve who was called "Little Douglas", a distant relation of the family at the castle. As may well be imagined, the greetings between Mary and her host and hostess were brief. The Queen was shown to her apartment on the first floor with windows looking out on the loch. She was soon left alone with Mary Seaton, the only one of the four Maries who was allowed to accompany her.

Brief as was the first meeting, and few and guarded as were the words which were exchanged between prisoner and gaolers, Mary had had time from what she knew in advance to form a reasonably exact idea of the new actors who were to play parts in her life's drama.

Lady Douglas was a woman aged between fifty-five and sixty. She had been beautiful enough in her youth to attract the favourable attention of James V by whom she had a son—the Murray who had already been so prominent a figure in Mary's life and whom, despite the fact that he was illegitimate, she always treated as a brother. For a brief while Murray's mother had cherished the hope of becoming the King's wife, his passion for her seemingly being deeply heartfelt. It was quite possible that her hope might have been fulfilled, for the family of Mar from which she was descended was one of the oldest and noblest in Scotland. But unfortunately for her, scandalmongering among the young noblemen of the day came to James' ears. It was rumoured that the beautiful favourite divided her favours between her royal lover and another whom she had taken from the lower orders of society, doubtless out of curiosity. It was further added that this particular person, Porterfield by name, was the real father of the child who had already been christened James Stuart, and whom the King was bringing up as his son at the Monastery of St Andrews.

These rumours, true or false, stopped James V at the moment when, in gratitude to her who had borne him a son, he was about to raise to the title of queen. Instead of marrying her, he suggested that she should choose a husband from among the nobles in his court. As she was beautiful and the King's favour was understood to accompany the marriage, Lord William Douglas, upon whom her choice fell, agreed to the marriage.

However, in spite of the protection which James V extended to her as long as he lived, Lady Douglas could never forget that she had once aspired to a much loftier rank. She had, in consequence, conceived a bitter hatred for the woman who in her eyes had usurped her place, and poor Mary as a matter of course inherited Lady Douglas' intense animosity towards her mother. This was shown in the few words the two women exchanged when they met. With age Lady Douglas, whether from repentance for her past failings or through hypocrisy, had become a prude and a puritan, so that at this period her natural acerbity of character was intensified by the rigid principles of the religion which she had adopted.

William Douglas, half-brother of Murray through his

mother, was a man of thirty-five or thirty-six, endowed with great physical strength, with rugged features, and red hair and beard like all of the younger branch of the family. He had inherited the deadly hatred which the Douglases had cherished for the Stuarts for the past century and which had for its fruits numberless conspiracies, rebellions and murders.

According as fortune smiled or frowned upon Murray, his own power had increased or diminished, and he had come to feel that his own life was dependent upon another's. Thus Mary's downfall which must inevitably result in Murray's elevation to power was a matter of self-congratulation. The confederate nobles could have made no better choice than to entrust the care of their prisoner to the instinctive rancour of Lady Douglas and the hatred of her son.

"Little Douglas" had been left an orphan some months before when he was twelve. He had been taken into the family at Lochleven where he was made to pay dearly for his adoption by the harshest of harsh treatment. The result was that the child, who had the Douglas pride and capacity for hatred, and knew that his birth was equal to that of his arrogant guardians, felt his weakness and isolation and locked up his thoughts within himself with a strength of character far beyond his years—the initial gratitude had changed to a lasting and intense bitterness. Apparently humble and submissive, he was biding his time until he should become a young man and could take his leave of Lochleven, and perhaps exact revenge for the insults which his relatives heaped upon him.

His feeling for revenge did not, however, extend to all the members of the family. The child's hatred for William Douglas and his mother was perhaps less deeply rooted than his love for George, the second of Lady Douglas's sons. George Douglas was absent from the castle when the Queen arrived. He was at this time about twenty-five or twenty-six years old. By a singular chance, which the scandals of his mother's early life led William Douglas to interpret unfavourably, this second son possessed none of the distinctive Douglas features—prominent cheekbones, large ears and red hair. George was naturally pale, with deep blue eyes, and black hair. Since his birth, he was an object of utter indifference to his father, and of hatred to his elder brother. So far as his mother was concerned, George had never been, so far as could be seen, given any particularly motherly love, whether because she was genuinely surprised at the striking variation in his features or because she knew the explanation of it and was ashamed.

As a result, the young man had been left to his own devices from childhood and had grown to full manhood like a wild shrub, full of strength and vigour but uncultivated and neglected. From his fifteenth year they had become accustomed to his unexplained absences and these could easily be accounted for by the indifference which everyone showed to him. He appeared at the castle only at rare intervals, rather like those migratory birds which always return to the same spot but remain there only for a brief time before flying away again to some other part of the world.

An instinctive consciousness of fellowship in misfortune drew George and "Little Douglas" together. When George saw how the child was ill-treated by everyone, he developed a strong friendship for him. When the boy felt the breath of love in the atmosphere of indifference which surrounded him he responded to George with open arms and heart. One day when the child had committed some trivial fault, and William Douglas had his dog-whip in the air to strike him, George, who was sitting deep in thought upon a rock, at once rushed at his brother, snatched the whip from his hand and threw it away.

At this William drew his sword, and George his. The two brothers, who had had the deadliest hatred of each other for twenty years, were on the point of killing each other. "Little Douglas" had picked up the whip and then knelt in front of William and handed it to him saying, "Strike me,

I deserve it." The child's intervention gave the young men time to reflect and, terrified at the crime they were likely to commit, and silently returning their swords to their scabbards, they separated. From that episode, new strength was given to the friendship between George and "Little Douglas" —indeed on the child's part it had grown to be downright worship.

Such was the family, minus George (who, as has been said, was absent when the Queen arrived) that Mary had come to live with. She had fallen suddenly from power to the state of a prisoner, for she had no doubt from the day after her arrival that that was her standing as an inmate of Lochleven Castle. On that morning Lady Douglas presented herself. With a badly disguised hatred under a pretence of respectful indifference, she requested Mary to go with her to inspect those parts of the castle which had been set aside for the Queen's personal use. She led her through three rooms, one of which was to be her bedroom, the second a sitting-room, and the third an antechamber. She then preceded the Queen down a spiral staircase leading to the great hall of the castle, its only outlet being into the garden. It was a small, square piece of ground laid out as a flower garden and with an ornamental fountain in the centre. There were also a few trees, the tops of which Mary had seen high above the wall when she first arrived. The garden was entered through a low doorway, and there was a similar one in an opposite wall which opened on to the loch. Like all the doors of the castle, the keys never left the belt or the bedside of William Douglas. The door was guarded day and night by a sentinel. This was her whole domain—she who had but yesterday had at her disposal palaces, and the plains and mountains of a whole kingdom.

When Mary returned to her rooms she found breakfast prepared and William Douglas standing by the table. He was there to carry out the duties of carver and taster for the Queen. Notwithstanding their bitter hatred for Mary the

Douglases would have felt themselves eternally disgraced if any mishap had befallen her while she was an inmate of their castle. It was in order to prevent any fears on Mary's part that William Douglas, as governor of the castle, undertook not only to carve the food in her presence but also to taste every dish served and even the water and various wines which were brought to her.

These precautions caused Mary more regret than reassurance for she realized that, if persisted in, all freedom of conversation at her table would be made impossible as long as she stayed in the castle. The purpose of these proceedings was too well meant for her to take offence. However, she resigned herself to his company, repulsive as it was to her. But from that day she cut her meals so short that the most protracted dinner during all the time she was at Lochleven never lasted longer than a quarter of an hour.

Two days after her arrival, as Mary took her seat for breakfast, she found a letter addressed to her lying on her plate, put there by William Douglas. She recognized Murray's handwriting and her first feeling was one of delight for her only hope now lay in this brother of hers to whom she had always been generous and good. She had raised him from being a prior at St Andrews to an earl, and had bestowed upon him the magnificent domains which were part of the former Earldom of Murray. But above all, she had granted or feigned to grant the pardon for his part in Rizzio's murder. Great was her astonishment, therefore, when opening the letter she found it filled with bitter reproaches for her conduct together with an exhortation to repent and the reiterated declaration that she would never regain her liberty. Murray ended his letter with the announcement that, despite his distaste for public life, he had been forced into accepting the Regency for her sake rather than for love of his country. This was the only way that he had of ending the ignominious proceedings which the nobles were determined to bring against her as chief accomplice in Darnley's murder.

The implication was that Mary's imprisonment was a great good fortune for which she ought to thank God, and a vast improvement upon the fate which would have been hers had he not interceded for her.

This letter was a thunder-clap for Mary. But, determined not to give her enemies an opportunity to exult over her discomfiture, she summoned all her self-control and turning towards William Douglas said,

"I presume, sir, that you are already aware of the news contained in this letter for, although we are not children of the same mother, the writer is as closely related to you as to me and he would hardly have written to one of us without writing to the other. Moreover, like a good son, he must have been in haste to inform his mother of the unexpected honours which have fallen on him."

"Yes, Madam, we learned yesterday that, happily for Scotland, my brother has been appointed Regent. And as his respect for his mother is only equalled by his devotion to his country we hope that he will repair all the wrongs which favourites of all ranks and all kinds have for five years inflicted upon both alike."

"Both as a dutiful son and courteous host it is not for you to go further back in the history of Scotland," Mary retorted, "and not to make a daughter blush for her father's faults. I have heard it said that the wrongs of which you complain are of an earlier date than that which you mentioned, and that King James V earlier had favourites of both sexes. It has been further said that some repaid his love as poorly as others his friendship. If, sir, you are badly informed on these matters there is one who can enlighten you if he is still living, a certain Portefeld or Porterfield. I am not sure which for I find it difficult in remembering and pronouncing the names of these common people. But your noble mother can give you details concerning him."

With these words Mary rose and, leaving Douglas crimson with rage, went back to her bedroom bolting the door behind her. She did not appear again during the day, but sat by her window from which she could at least enjoy the magnificent view which included the plain and the village of Kinross. But the vast extent of the country which lay before her only intensified her depression when her eyes wandered back from the horizon to the foot of the castle with its high walls surrounded on all sides by the deep waters of the loch. On the surface, nothing could be seen but a single boat from which "Little Douglas" was fishing.

For some minutes Mary had been gazing abstractedly at the child when, suddenly, a horn sounded from the direction of Kinross. The boy at once pulled in his line and rowed in the direction from which the signal came with a skill and strength seemingly beyond his years. Mary followed him with a listless gaze as he pulled to a part of the shore so distant that the boat dwindled to an almost imperceptible speck. But presently it reappeared, increasing rapidly in size. She saw that it was bringing a passenger to the castle, a passenger wielding the oars so skilfully that the little boat fairly flew over the tranquil water, leaving in its wake ripples which danced in the rays of the setting sun.

Skimming along with the swiftness of a bird, the boat was soon so near that Mary could see that the sturdy rower was a young man of about twenty-five with long, black hair, wearing a green doublet and a mountaineer's cap with an eagle's feather. As he came nearer, his back being towards the castle, the boy leaned towards him and said a few words which made him at once turn and look towards the Queen. Instinctively she drew back from the window, but not so quickly that she did not catch a glimpse of the handsome, pale face of the stranger. When she returned to the window he had passed out of sight behind a corner of the castle.

Everything is subject to conjecture by a prisoner, and it seemed to Mary that the stranger's face was familiar. However, search her memory as she would, she could recall nothing definite and she finally decided that she had been

84

deceived by some vague and indistinct resemblance to someone else.

And yet, strive as she might, the idea had taken a firm hold in her mind. She had continually before her eyes the little boat skimming over the water with the young man and the child aboard as if they were coming to her rescue. Although there was nothing positive in these prisoner's fancies she slept more peacefully that night than she had done since her arrival at Lochleven.

When she got up the next morning, Mary ran to her window. The weather was beautiful and everything seemed to smile on her: water, sky, and land. Without understanding her own motives she decided not to go down into the garden before breakfast. When the door opened she turned quickly around. William Douglas was there as usual to perform his duty of taster. The meal was brief and eaten in silence. As soon as Douglas went out, Mary left her tower. As she passed through the great hall she saw two horses standing saddled before the door, indicating the approaching departure of a man and his groom. Was the black-haired young man to take his leave so soon? Mary neither dared nor wished to ask the question. She kept on her way to the garden and as she entered she saw at a glance that it was deserted.

She strolled about for a few minutes, but soon wearied of it and returned to her rooms. As she passed through the hall once again she saw that the horses had gone. Immediately she was upstairs she hurried to the window to see if she could see anything on the loch which might enlighten her. She saw a boat moving away from the island and on board were the two horses and their riders, one of whom was William Douglas and the other a family servant.

Mary followed the boat until it touched the shore. There the travellers disembarked, leading their horses. They then galloped off taking the same route by which the Queen had come. Since the horses were completely covered with trappings Mary assumed that Douglas was on his way to Edinburgh. As soon as it had landed its passengers, the boat returned to the castle.

At that moment, Mary Seaton announced that Lady Douglas sought permission to call on the Queen.

It was only the second time that the two women found themselves face to face after many years of hatred on the part of Lady Douglas and contemptuous indifference on the Queen's part. With the instinctive artfulness which leads women under any circumstances to appear beautiful, especially to other women, Mary motioned with her hand to Mary Seaton and stood before a small mirror hanging on the wall in a heavy gothic frame. She arranged her hair and adjusted the lace about her neck. She sat down in a graceful attitude in the only armchair which the room could boast. Only then did she say smilingly to Mary Seaton that she might admit the visitor, who came in immediately.

Mary's expectation was not disappointed. In spite of her loathing for James V's daughter, and in spite of the self-control which she believed she possessed, Lady Douglas could not suppress a gesture of amazement at the sight of Mary's marvellous beauty. She had expected to find her crushed by her misfortunes, pale from tiredness, and humbled by captivity, but she remained the calm, beautiful, and haughty creature of before. Mary saw the effect she had produced, and with an ironical smile, partly to Mary Seaton who was leaning on the back of her chair and partly to her unexpected visitor, said,

"We are fortunate today, for it would seem we are allowed to enjoy the company of our good hostess to whom we must express our gratefulness for her observance of the empty ceremonial of announcing her visit, which she might easily have dispensed with having the keys of our rooms."

"If my calling is inopportune to Your Grace," Lady Douglas replied, "I regret it the more because circumstances make it my duty to call upon you twice daily, at least during the absence of my son who has been summoned to Edinburgh by the Regent. It was of this that I came to inform Your Grace, not with the empty ceremony which obtains at court but simply with the courtesy which I owe to every person who has the hospitality of this castle."

"Our good hostess misunderstands us," Mary rejoined with affected affability, "but the Regent himself can bear witness to the pleasure we have always taken in the companionship of all who remind us, however indirectly, of our well-beloved father James V. Lady Douglas, therefore, does us wrong by attributing our surprise at her unlooked for appearance to chagrin or discourtesy, and the hospitality which she so courteously proffers does not promise, in spite of her goodwill, sufficient distraction for us to deprive ourselves of that which her visits cannot fail to give us."

"Unhappily, Madam," retorted Lady Douglas, whom Mary had kept standing before her, "great as is the pleasure which I derive from these visits I shall be compelled to forego them except at mealtimes. I am now too old to endure fatigue, and have always been too proud to submit to sarcasm."

"Really, Seaton," Mary exclaimed as if surprised at her negligence, "we had forgotten that Lady Douglas having acquired the right to sit in the presence of the King, my father, ought surely to enjoy the right in the prison of the Queen, his daughter. Bring a stool, Seaton, that our failure of memory may not deprive us of our amiable hostess's company. Or," she continued, rising and indicating her own chair to Lady Douglas who was preparing to leave, "if a stool does not suit your ladyship, take this armchair—you will not be the first of your family to sit in my place."

To this last allusion to Mary's usurpation Lady Douglas was doubtless about to make a bitter reply when the young man with the black hair appeared unannounced at the door. He advanced towards Lady Douglas without any gesture of respect for Mary.

"Madam," he said, bowing, "the boat which put my brother ashore has just returned and one of the men who accompanied him was entrusted with an urgent message for you which William forgot to give you himself."

With that he saluted the old lady respectfully again and at once left the room without so much as looking towards the Queen, who was deeply wounded by this lack of respect. She turned to Mary Seaton and with her usual calmness of manner said,

"Who told us, Seaton, of certain rumours which were derogatory to our hostess's reputation and good name about a youth with pale cheeks and black hair? If the man who has just left us was, as I have every reason to believe, that same youth I am ready to assure all doubters that he is a genuine Douglas, not in the manner of courage of which I have no proof, but in the manner of insolence of which he has just given us abundant proof. Come, my little one, let us leave the room," the Queen continued, leaning on Mary Seaton's arm, "for our kind hostess may be obliged by courtesy to keep us company for a longer time and we know that she is impatiently awaited elsewhere."

With these words, Mary went into her bedroom while the old lady, utterly confused by the flood of sarcasm which the Queen had poured on her, left the room muttering, "Yes, yes, he is a Douglas, and with God's help I hope to prove it."

The Queen's strength held up so long as it was sustained by her enemy's presence, but the moment she was left with no other witness of her weakness than Mary Seaton, she collapsed on to a chair and wept bitterly. She had been cruelly hurt, for until that day no man except Ruthven had ever come near her without doing homage to her as Queen or to her beauty. And what had happened—the very man upon whom she had instinctively founded hopes of freedom had insulted her twice over, both as a Queen and a woman. She remained in her room until evening.

When the time for dinner came Lady Douglas climbed the

stairs to Mary's room. Lady Douglas was dressed in her handsomest gown and was followed by four servants carrying the different dishes composing the prisoners' meal. These were followed by the old steward of the castle with his gold chain of office around his neck and his ivory cane in his hand, as on ceremonial occasions. The servants put the dishes on the table and waited in silence for the Queen to appear. But when the bedroom door opened it was to admit Mary Seaton instead of the Queen.

"Madam," she said, "my mistress has not been well during the day and will eat nothing this evening. It will be useless, therefore, for you to wait longer."

"Allow me to hope," Lady Douglas replied, "that she may change her mind. In any event, you can bear witness that I have carried out my duty."

A servant then handed her bread and salt on a silver tray, while the steward, who acted as carver in William Douglas' absence, served her with a small portion of each of the dishes on the table. When this formality was ended, "So the Queen will not appear again today?" Lady Douglas inquired.

"That is Her Majesty's determination."

"In that case," returned the old lady, "our presence here is useless. But the dinner is served, and should Her Grace need anything she has only to call out."

She then withdrew with the same unbending dignity as when she had entered, followed by the servants and the steward.

As Lady Douglas had foreseen, the Queen finally yielded to Mary Seaton's entreaties and left her room at about eight in the evening. She sat at the table and, waited on by her only remaining lady of honour, ate sparingly. Then she rose and went to the window.

It was one of those superb summer late evenings when all nature seemed to rejoice. The sky was studded with early stars which were reflected in the loch. Among their reflections, like a star of greater brilliance, shone the flame of a torch at the stern of a small boat. By the light which it shed the Queen could recognize George and "Little Douglas" fishing. Despite her longing to take advantage of the lovely late evening and to breathe in the pure air, the sight of this young man whose conduct had so outraged her during the day affected her so much that she at once closed the window and returned to her bedroom. She lay down and asked her companion in captivity to read some prayers to her. She was so agitated she could not sleep and, getting up again and throwing on a dressing-gown, she returned to her seat at the window. The boat had vanished.

For the greater part of the night Mary sat gazing abstractedly at the immensity of the sky or across the dark waters of the loch. Despite the agitation in her brain she felt tremendous physical relief from breathing the fresh air and the contemplation of the peaceful, silent night. The result was, when she did waken the next morning, she was more tranquil and resigned. But, unfortunately, the sight of Lady Douglas who made her appearance at breakfast time to carry out her duties as taster brought back all her irritability. Perhaps, nevertheless, matters might have passed off smoothly if Lady Douglas had left after tasting the different dishes instead of remaining standing by the buffet. But her persistence in standing thus throughout the meal, even although it may really have been intended as a mark of respect, seemed to the Queen an intolerable tyranny.

"Little one," she said to Mary Seaton, "have you so soon forgotten that our excellent hostess complained yesterday that it tired her to stand? Bring one of the two stools which furnish our royal apartment, and be careful that it is not the one with the broken leg."

"If the furnishings of Lochleven Castle are in such a bad state, Madam," the old lady replied, "it is the fault of the kings of Scotland. The poor Douglases have had so little share in their favour that they have been unable to maintain the splendid establishments of their ancestors, or even to compete with ordinary commoners. I am told there was once a musician at the court who spent more than their yearly income in a single month."

"Those who are so expert in helping themselves, my lady," rejoined the Queen, "stand in no need of gifts. It seems to me that the Douglases have lost nothing by waiting and there is not a younger son of that illustrious family who may not now aspire to the most eminent marriage. Truly, it is a pity that our sister the Queen of England has, so it is said, sworn to remain a virgin."

"Or that the Queen of Scotland is not for the third time a widow," snapped Lady Douglas. "However," she continued, as if suddenly remembering to whom she spoke, "I do not say that by way of reproach to Your Grace for Catholics regard marriage as a sacrament and as such receive it as often as possible."

"And there lies the difference between them and Protestants," Mary retorted, "for they have not equal respect for it and therefore think that in certain circumstances they are justified in dispensing with it altogether."

At this terrible piece of sarcasm Lady Douglas took a step towards the Queen, holding a knife which she had just used to cut off a piece of meat for tasting. But the Queen rose and faced her so calmly and majestically that involuntary respect, or shame for first impulse, made her drop the weapon. Unable to think of words strong enough to express what she felt she signalled to the servants to follow her and left the room with as much dignity as her anger allowed.

As soon as the door closed behind her, Mary resumed her seat, smiling with happiness and triumph at her victory. She ate with better appetite than she had done since she became a prisoner, while Mary Seaton, in an undertone and with every possible respect, deplored the fatal gift of satire with which Mary had been born, and which, with her beauty, was one of the prime causes of her misfortunes. But the Queen laughed at her and said that she was curious to see how her hostess would conduct herself at dinner that evening.

After breakfast Mary went down to the garden. The gratification of her pride had partly restored her normal good humour. She noticed a mandoline lying on a chair in the great hall as they passed through and asked Mary Seaton to pick it up so that she might see, she said, whether she still kept her former talent. She was, in fact, one of the most accomplished musicians of her time and, according to Brantôme, played admirably both the lute and the 'viole d'amour', an instrument closely resembling the mandoline.

When they reached the garden the Queen sat down in the darkest corner of the grove of trees. Having tuned her instrument, she began to touch the strings quickly and lightly. Little by little, the chords she struck became mournful. At the same time her face assumed an expression of great sadness. Even although she had long been accustomed to these sudden changes of mood in her mistress, Mary Seaton watched her anxiously, and she was about to ask the reason for her sudden gloom when Mary began to sing in a low voice and as if for her own ear alone the following verses:

Caves, meadows, mountains, plains, rocks, woods and forests, streams, rivers, fountains, where I stray alone with vague complaints and tears that overflow, I long to sing of the wretched grief that makes me lament so.

But who will hear my heavy sigh? Who will understand my ennui and languor? Will it be this grass or reed, or the water flowing by, which as it flows, bears the tears from my eyes?

Hélas! No, vainly does my wounded heart seek the healing balm in things that cannot heal. Much better should my pain bitterly complain to the ears of him who has brought this torture on my soul.

Oh, thou immortal goddess, pray listen to my voice, thou who makes me lie weak beneath thy sway, so that

if my life must know its end by thy blow then thy cruelty
killed at thine own behest.

Tis plain, all men may see my face slowly pine away
like cold ice near the fire's heat; yet the burning ray
which scorches and consumes me wakens no display of
pity for my woe.

And yet these trees which stand about me, and every
rocky wall, these my sorrow know and see. And so, in
brief, all nature knows my sorry plight and thou alone
feeds on my cruel torment

But should it be thy will to see me, wretched me
torment still, then let my woeful ill everlasting be.

The last verse was scarcely audible. It was as if the Queen
were at the end of her strength. The mandoline slipped from
her hands and would have fallen to the ground if Mary
Seaton had not bent quickly down and caught it. She knelt
for some time at her mistress's feet, silently gazing at her.
Seeing that the Queen was sinking deeper and deeper into a
gloomy withdrawal she asked hesitatingly, "Did those
verses recall sad memories to Your Majesty?"

"Yes, they recalled to me the unhappy young man who
wrote them."

"Without impertinence may I ask who was the author?"

"Hélas! He was a noble, gallant, and handsome young
man, devoted and impulsive, who would be protecting me
today had I protected him when I could have done. But his
impulsiveness was reckless, and his fault a crime. What would
you do? I did not love him. But poor Chatelard, I was very
cruel to him."

"But it was not you who brought him to trial. It was your
brother. The judges condemned him, not you."

"Yes, yes, I know that he was one of Murray's victims and
doubtless that was why the thought of him came to me.
But I might have been able to have had him pardoned, little
one, and I was unyielding. I allowed a man whose only

93

crime was that he loved me too well to go to the scaffold. And now I wonder and repine because I am abandoned by everyone. Listen. There is one thing that terrifies me: when I search my conscience I find that not only have I deserved what has befallen me, but that God does not punish me severely enough."

"Such ideas as those will drive you mad, Your Grace," Mary Seaton cried, "and look at the state those wretched verses have brought you to, verses which came into your mind today just when you were beginning to be yourself once more."

"Hélas," the Queen replied, shaking her head and sighing deeply, "in the last six years there have been few days when I have not repeated those verses to myself, although today is the first time that I have repeated them aloud. He was French and they have banished, imprisoned or killed all those who came with me from France. Do you remember the ship which sank before our eyes as we sailed from Calais? I cried out then that it was a bad omen, and everyone tried to reassure me. Now tell me, who was right, they or me?"

The Queen had fallen into one of those fits of melancholy for which tears are the only cure. Mary Seaton, realizing that any attempt to console her would not only be inopportune but useless fell in with her mistress's mood instead of struggling with it. The result was that the Queen whose sobs were stifling her at last wept freely and was solaced. Little by little she recovered her self-control and the crisis passed, leaving her, as such crises always did, more resolute than ever. When she returned to her rooms it was impossible to read on her face the slightest trace of emotion.

The time for dinner was approaching and Mary, who in the morning had waited for it with impatience after her triumph over Lady Douglas, now looked forward to it with some uneasiness. The mere thought of coming face to face again with that woman whose pride she had constantly to defeat by sarcasm wearied her further after the nervous fatigue of the day. She therefore decided to do what she had done the previous evening and not appear for dinner. She was the more inclined to congratulate herself on her decision when she learned that on this particular occasion the tasting duties were to be carried out not by Lady Douglas but by George Douglas. His mother, still upset by that morning's scene, had sent him to replace her. When Mary Seaton told the Queen that she had seen the black-haired young man crossing the hall on his way to their rooms Mary was, indeed, well satisfied with the course she had adopted, for his impertinence had wounded her more deeply than all the overbearing insolence of his mother.

The Queen was more than a little astonished, therefore, when a few minutes later Mary Seaton came to her room to tell her that George Douglas had dismissed the servants and begged the honour of talking to her on an important matter. At first the Queen refused to see him, but her lady-in-waiting said that the young man's manner and bearing were so different from what they had been previously that she thought her mistress would be wrong if she refused his request. Mary got up and entered the adjoining room with the dignity natural to her and, having taken a few steps beyond the door, stopped and waited disdainfully for him to address her.

Mary Seaton had spoken truly. George Douglas was not the overbearing and insolent creature of the previous occasion, but respectful and almost timid. He made a movement towards the Queen but checked himself when he saw that Mary Seaton stood behind her.

"Madam," he said, "I particularly wish to speak with Her Majesty alone. Will she not grant me that favour?"

"Mary Seaton's presence, sir, need be no restraint, for she is my sister and my friend, and more than that, she is the companion of my captivity."

"And in each of these capacities, Madam, she has my greatest respect. But what I have to say to Your Majesty must be heard by no ears but yours, and as another opportunity may not present itself I implore you in the name of all you hold dear to grant what I ask."

There was such a note of entreaty, such respectful sincerity in his voice, that Mary turned towards her companion and said with an affectionate gesture,

"Go, little one; but have no fear, you will lose nothing by not hearing. Go."

Mary Seaton withdrew, the Queen following her with smiling eyes until the door closed behind her. She then turned to George.

"Now that we are alone, sir, speak."

But George Douglas, instead of replying walked towards her, and knelt. As he did so, he took a paper from his breast which he handed to her. Mary took it with astonishment. As she unfolded it, she gazed fixedly at Douglas, who still knelt. She then read the following declaration:

We, peers of Scotland, in consideration of the fact that our Queen is held prisoner at Lochleven and that her faithful subjects are denied access to her person, and believing it our duty to take measures to assure her safety, do promise and swear to use every reasonable means in our power to set her at liberty on considerations compatible with Her Majesty's honour, the welfare of the kingdom, and to guarantee the lives of those who hold her in prison provided they consent to release her; should they refuse we declare that we propose to devote ourselves and our children, friends, servants, and vassals, our property and our lives, to secure her liberty, to assure the safety of the Prince, and to press forward the punishment of the murderers of the late consort of the Queen. If we are attacked because of our intentions, either as a body or individually, we swear to defend ourselves and to aid one another, or to confess ourselves infamous and perjured. May God help us.

Signed with our hands at Dumbarton:
 Andrews, Argyle, Huntly, Arbroath, Galloway, Ross,
 Fleming, Herries, Stirling, Kilwinning, Wilt [sic], Hamil-
 ton, and Saint-Clair, chevalier.

"And Seaton!" Mary exclaimed. "Among these signatures I do not see that of my faithful Seaton."

Still kneeling, Douglas drew another paper from his
breast and handed it to her with the same marks of respect.
It contained only these few words:

 Trust George Douglas, for Your Majesty has no more
 devoted friend in all your kingdom.

Seaton.

Mary looked down into Douglas's face with an expression
which belonged to her alone. Then she held out her hand to
help him rise.

"Ah!" she said with a sign in which there was more joy
than sadness, "I see that despite my mistakes, God has not
yet abandoned me. But how can it be that you, a Douglas . . .
Oh, I cannot believe it!"

"Madam, seven years have passed since I first saw you in
France, and seven years have passed since I began to love
you."

Mary gave a start, but Douglas put out his hand and
shook his head with an expression of such humility that she
saw she could safely listen to what he had to say.

"Rest assured, Madam," he continued, "I should never
have made this confession did it not explain my conduct and
show you why I may be trusted. Yes, I have loved you for
seven years, but as one loves a star one does not hope to reach
or a Madonna to whom one can only pray. For seven years
I have followed you everywhere without so much as a
glance from you, and without attempting by word or deed
to attract your attention. I was on the Chevalier de Mévillon's
galley when you came to Scotland; I was among the Regent's
troops when you fought with Huntly; I was one of your
escort when you went to visit Lord Darnley at Glasgow

during his illness; I reached Edinburgh an hour after your departure for Lochleven. Then, for the first time, it seemed to me that my true mission was revealed to me and I knew that the love with which I had until then reproached myself as a crime was, in fact, a signal mark of God's favour. I learned that the nobles were assembled at Dumbarton and I hurried there. I pledged my name, my honour, and my life, and I obtained from them, because of the ease with which I can pass in and out of this castle, the privilege of bringing to you the document they had just signed. Now, Madam, forget all that I have just said, except the assurance of my devotion and deference. Forget that I am near you. I am used to obscurity, but if you need me you have but to make a sign, for I am at your service."

"Hélas!" Mary exclaimed, "this morning I complained that no one loved me. I ought rather to bewail the fact that I am still beloved, for the love I inspire is fatal. Look back, Douglas, and count the graves that, young as I am, I have left along my path, François II, Chatelard, Rizzio, Darnley . . . Ah, it must be something stronger than love which leads you to stay beside me now. It must be true heroism and devotion, and all the more so, Douglas, because as you yourself have said your love can have no possible reward—you understand that?"

"Madam, Madam," said Douglas, "am I not more than rewarded by being able to see you every day, by the hope that through me you will regain your liberty and that, if I cannot set you free, I shall at least die in your service."

"Poor boy," Mary murmured, closing her eyes as if she foresaw the fate which awaited her new champion.

"Say rather 'Happy Douglas'," he replied, taking the Queen's hand and kissing it, "'Happy Douglas' for he has already obtained from Your Majesty more than he had dared to hope—a sigh."

"What did you and your friends decide?" the Queen asked, raising him again from his knees.

"Nothing as yet, Madam, for we have scarcely had time to confer. Your escape, which would be impossible without me, will be very difficult even with my help. Your Majesty has seen that it was necessary for me to treat you with utter disrespect before my mother in order to win the confidence which has enabled me to see you today. If that confidence on my mother's part, or my brother's, ever reaches the point that they entrust me with the castle keys, then your escape is assured. But Your Majesty must be surprised at nothing. In public I shall always be a Douglas—that is to say your enemy—and unless your life be in danger I shall not say a word nor make a gesture which would betray my devotion to you. But I do implore you to remember that present or absent, whether I keep silent or speak, whether I am idle or active, my devotion is unchanging and unchangeable. Look in that direction every evening," he continued, walking to the window and pointing to a small house on the hill of Kinross, "and so long as you see a light shining there you will know that your friends are watching over you, and that you must not lose hope."

"My thanks, Douglas, my thanks. It inspires me with fresh courage to meet a heart like yours."

"And now I must take leave of Your Majesty. To stay longer with you would be to arouse suspicion, and a single whisper of suspicion about my trustworthiness and that light, which is your only beacon of hope, would be extinguished and all would be night again."

With these words George Douglas bowed more respectfully than he had done before and withdrew. He left Mary with her heart filled with hope and gratified pride—for the homage which had been tendered to her had been to the woman rather than to the Queen.

As the Queen had promised her it was not long before Mary Seaton knew everything, even Douglas's love for her. The two women impatiently awaited the coming of darkness to see if the promised star shone in the distance. They were not disappointed. As soon as night fell the light appeared and the Queen trembled with joy. Her companion could not induce her to leave the window where she sat with her eyes fixed on the little house at Kinross. At last she yielded to Mary Seaton's entreaties to go to bed, but twice during the night she got up and went quietly to the window. The light was always burning, and disappeared only at dawn with its sisters the stars.

At breakfast the next morning George Douglas announced to the Queen his brother William's return. He would be arriving that same evening, and George would be leaving Lochleven the following morning to confer with the nobles who had signed the declaration and who had separated at once to raise troops in their respective territories. The Queen could not, with any success, attempt flight until she could be assured that an army strong enough had been formed to take the field. So far as George Douglas was concerned his silent disappearances and unexpected returns were so customary that there was no reason to fear that his departure would arouse any suspicion.

Chapter 7

Everything happened as George Douglas had said. That evening a blast on a horn announced William's return. He was accompanied by Lord Ruthven, whose father had taken so prominent a part in Rizzio's murder and who had died in exile in England of the disease which had afflicted him before that event. The two came in advance of Lord Lindsay of Byres and Sir Robert Melville, brother of Mary's former ambassador to England. These three were entrusted on behalf of the Regent with a mission to the Queen.

And so the old order was restored, with William Douglas resuming his duties as carver. Breakfast was over and Mary had heard nothing of George's departure or Ruthven's arrival. When she left the table she went to the window. She had hardly reached it when she heard the horn ring out from the shore and saw a small troop of horsemen waiting for the boat to come and take off those who were visiting the castle.

The distance was too great for her to recognize any of the party, but it was clear enough from the signals that were being exchanged between the little troop and the occupants of the castle that the newcomers were her enemies. In her uneasiness the Queen did not let her eyes leave the boat which went over to fetch them. She saw that only two men came aboard, and the boat immediately started back to the castle.

As the craft drew nearer Mary's forebodings changed to downright fear, for in one of the newcomers she though she recognized Lord Lindsay, who had escorted her to Lochleven a week previously. It was indeed he. He wore his usual visorless helmet which left exposed the harsh features which betrayed his violent nature. His long, black beard sprinkled with grey fell down to reach his chest. His body was protected, as in battle, by a cuirass which had once been well-polished and gilded but which, through incessant exposure to rain and fog, was now eaten with rust. He carried on his back a huge sword as one might wear a quiver. It was so heavy that both hands were needed to wield it, and so long that the hilt touched his left shoulder and the point reached to his right spur. In a word, he was always the soldier, brave to foolhardiness, rough and insolent, and always ready to resort to brute force when he believed himself in the right.

The Queen was so engrossed by the sight of Lindsay that she neglected, until the boat was about to land, to glance at his companion. She then recognized Sir Robert Melville. This gave her some consolation for she knew that whatever might happen she could be sure of his secret sympathy, though he dared not show it. His style of dress, too, by which one can form an opinion of a man (as it was possible to form an opinion of Lord Lindsay by his) was in striking contrast to that of his companion. He wore a black velvet doublet with a cap and plume of the same colour, the plume being held in place by a gold clasp; his only weapon, offensive and defensive, was a short sword which seemed to be carried rather to indicate his rank than for any fighting purpose. His features and bearing were in keeping with his unwarlike dress; the pale face showed shrewdness and intelligence; the eyes were kind, and the voice was gentle and winning. His figure was slender and he stooped slightly, rather from habit than years, for at this time he was only forty-five.

The presence of this peaceable man, however, whose mission was probably to keep an eye on Lindsay, did not entirely reassured the Queen. As the boat passed out of sight around a corner of one of the towers in order to reach the landing-place in front of the main gateway she asked Mary Seaton to go downstairs and try to find out what had brought

Lindsay to Lochleven. She had sufficient confidence in her own strength of will to feel sure that a few moments' preparation, whatever the motive of his visit might be, would be sufficient for her to compose her face and to assume that calm and majesty which had always so deeply impressed her enemies.

Left alone, Mary turned her eyes on the little house at Kinross wherein lay her only hope, but the distance was too great for her to distinguish anything. Moreover, the shutters were closed all day and opened only in the evening, rather like clouds having hidden the sun during the day moved apart at night to allow the lost sailor to see his pole-star. Yet she stood there immobile, her eyes fixed on the same spot, when Mary Seaton's returning footsteps roused her from her rapt contemplation.

"Well, little one?" she asked, turning towards the door.

"Your Majesty was not mistaken. It was indeed Sir Robert Melville and Lord Lindsay who arrived, but a third emissary came yesterday with William Douglas whose name I greatly fear is much more hateful to you than either of the others."

"You are wrong, Mary. Neither Melville's name nor Lindsay's is hateful to me. On the contrary the name of Melville in my present circumstances is one which gives me the greatest pleasure to hear. While Lord Lindsay's name has not the same welcoming sound, it is still an honourable one and always borne by men, rough and ill-mannered certainly, but incapable of treason. But tell me, for you see that I am calm and prepared to hear it, what is this other name?"

"Hélas, Madam, calm and prepared though you may well be, summon all your courage, for not only must you hear the name pronounced but in a few moments you must receive the man who bears it—Lord Ruthven."

She spoke truly. The name had a terrible effect on Mary. It had hardly been uttered when she gave a shriek and clung to the casement for support, turning pale as death. Mary Seaton, alarmed at the effect of the hated name, rushed to her side to support her, but the Queen held out a hand to stop her and pressed the other against her heart.

"It is nothing," the Queen said, "in a moment I will be myself again. Yes, Mary, you were right, that is a fatal name inseparably connected with my most bitter memories. The demand which these men have come to make is certain to be one of terrible consequence. But never mind, soon I will be ready to receive my brother's emissaries, for, without any doubt, they come in his name. You, little one, see that they do not enter, for I must have a few moments to recover my wits. You know it will not be long."

With that the Queen walked with steady steps to her bedroom.

Mary Seaton was left alone, marvelling at the strength of mind which made Mary Stuart, who was such a woman through and through, a man when danger approached. She went at once to the door to secure it with a wooden bar which passed through two iron rings. But the bar had been taken away, so that there was no way to secure the door from the inside. A moment later she heard someone coming up the stairs. Guessing by the heavy, echoing step that it was Lindsay, she looked about her to see if she could find anything to replace the bar. Nothing was at hand so she put her arm through the rings, determined to let it be broken rather than allow her mistress to be disturbed one minute before it suited her convenience. As soon as the steps reached the landing someone knocked violently on the door and a harsh voice called out,

"Come, open the door! Open it at once!"

"By what right," demanded Mary Seaton, "do you insolently order me to open the door of the Queen of Scotland?"

"By the right which the Regent's emissary has to enter anywhere in his name. I am Lord Lindsay and I have come to speak to Lady Mary Stuart."

"An emissary," Mary Seaton retorted, "is not exempt

from announcing his visit to a lady, and with stronger reason to a Queen. And although the emissary be, as he says, Lord Lindsay, he will await his sovereign's pleasure as every well-born Scot would do in his place."

"By Saint Andrew! Open this door or I will break it down."

"Do nothing of the sort, my lord, I beg you," said another voice which Mary Seaton recognized as Melville's. "Let us wait for a moment for Lord Ruthven who is not yet ready."

"Upon my soul!" Lindsay cried, violently shaking the door, "I will not wait a second." Then as the door resisted his efforts he said to a servant, "Did you not tell me, fool, that the bar had been taken away?"

"And so it has, my lord," was the reply.

"Then what has this hussy barred it with?"

"With my arm, my lord, which I have thrust through the rings, just as a Douglas did for James I in the days when the Douglases had black hair instead of red and were faithful subjects instead of traitors."

"As you know your history so well you should remember," Lindsay savagely replied, "that that weak barrier failed to stop Graham, and that Catherine Douglas's arm was broken like a stick and James I killed like a dog."

"And you, my lord," the courageous girl answered, "should be familiar with the ballad which has come down to this day:

> Now disgraced be Robert Graham,
> Assassin of the King,
> May all men curse this dastard
> Who did this wicked thing."

"Mary," called out the Queen who had heard the dispute from her bedroom, "open the door at once. Do you hear me?"

Mary Seaton obeyed and Lindsay entered, followed by Melville with lowered head and slow steps. Half-way across the second room of the apartment, Lindsay stopped and looked about him.

"Well, where is she?" he asked. "Has she not kept us waiting long enough outside that she keeps us waiting here? Or does she imagine that she is still Queen in spite of these walls and barriers?"

"Be patient, my lord," Melville murmured, "Lord Ruthven is not yet here and since we can do nothing without him let us await his arrival."

"Those who like can wait," Linsday snarled, aflame with indignation, "I will wait for no one, and wherever she may be I will seek her out."

As he spoke he took several steps towards Mary's bedroom, but at that moment the Queen opened the door, apparently unmoved either by the visit or the visitor's overbearing rudeness. She was so beautiful, so serenely dignified, that even Lindsay was awed to silence and bowed respectfully as if in obedience to a superior power.

"We fear we have kept you waiting, my Lord Lindsay," said the Queen, without any acknowledgement of the emissaries' salutes other than a slight inclination of her head, "but a woman does not willingly receive even her enemies without some attention to her appearance. Men, it is true, are less punctilious in that respect," she added, glancing at Lindsay's rusted armour and travel-stained and torn doublet. "Good day, Melville," she continued, disregarding Lindsay's muttered apologies, "welcome to our prison as you were welcome to our palace, for in either place, I believe you to be my faithful subject."

Then she turned again to Lindsay who was impatiently watching the door for Ruthven to appear, "You have there, my lord," pointing to the sword which was slung across his shoulder, "a faithful if rather weighty travelling companion. Did you expect to find enemies here against whom to use it? If not, it is a strange adornment with which to appear before a woman. However, I am too thoroughly a Stuart to fear the sight of a sword, even though it be a naked one."

"It is not out of place here, Madam," Lindsay replied, bringing the weapon round in front of him with the point on the ground and resting his elbow on the hilt, "for it is an old acquaintance of your family."

"Your ancestors, my lord, were so brave and so loyal that it is not for me to question the truth of your statement, and so good a blade must have rendered good service."

"Yes, Madam, that it did, but of a kind kings never pardon. He who ordered this sword to be made was Archibald 'Bell-the-cat' and he first wore it on the day when, to justify his name, he dragged from your grandfather, James III's, tent, his fawning favourites whom he hanged on the bridge at Lauder with the halters of his soldiers' horses. With the same sword he killed, with one blow in single combat, Spens of Kilspendie who had insulted him in the presence of James IV, trusting to the protection of his master which shielded him no better than his buckler which was slashed in two. Upon its owner's death two years later, after the defeat of Flodden where he left both his sons and two hundred warriors bearing the Douglas name upon the field, it passed to the Earl of Angus who drew it when he hunted the Hamiltons out of Edinburgh. This he did so quickly and so thoroughly that the affair was called the sweeping of the dirt from the streets. Finally, James V, your father, saw its glitter at the battle of the Bridge of the Tweed when Buccleuch, incited by him, tried to snatch him from the tutelage of the Douglases, and twenty-four warriors with the name of Scott were left on the field of battle."

"But how happens it," said the Queen, "that such a weapon did not remain as a family trophy with the Douglas? The Earl of Angus must have had good reason for parting with this modern Excalibur to you."

"Yes, without doubt, Madam, he had an excellent reason for giving it to me," Lindsay answered, ignoring Melville's gestures of entreaty, "and this part of the sword's history will interest you more than all the rest. Being so near our own days, you will readily recall the circumstances. It was only ten days ago upon the field of Carberry Hill when that infamous traitor Bothwell had the audacity to challenge to single combat any man who dared assert that he was guilty of your husband's murder. I was the third to tell him to his face that he was a murderer, and as he refused to fight with the two others under the pretext that they were only barons I, who am an earl, came forward in my turn. It was then that the noble Earl of Morton gave me this good sword that I might fight him to the death. Had his presumption been a little greater, or his cowardice a little less, I would have done such good work with this sword that the dogs and carrion crows would have feasted on that traitor's carcass."

At these words Mary Seaton and Sir Robert Melville gazed at each other aghast, for the events which Lindsay recalled were, indeed, so recent that they were still living in the Queen's heart. But she, with incredible calmness and with a scornful smile, replied,

"It is easy, my lord, to kill an enemy who does not enter the lists. But, believe me, if I had inherited my father's sword as well as his sceptre, your sword, long as it is, might have proved too short. But as your business with us at this moment, my lord, is to tell us what you propose doing rather than what you would have done earlier, we ask your pardon if we bring your mind back to something of more real interest, for it seems to us that you did not come here to add a chapter to Monsieur de Brantôme's little treatise *Des rodomontades Espagnoles*."

"You are right, Madam," Lindsay answered, flushed with anger, "and you would already know the purpose of the mission if Lord Ruthven did not keep us waiting for such an unconscionable time. But be patient, it will not be long for I hear him coming now."

Steps could, indeed, be heard climbing the stairs and approaching the room. At their sound the Queen, who had endured Lindsay's insults with so much spirit, paled visibly. Melville, who had not taken his eyes from her face, put out his hand towards her armchair as if to force her into it. But she motioned to him that there was no need and, to all appearances perfectly calm, she fixed her eyes upon the door. Ruthven appeared. It was the first time Mary had seen him since his father had murdered Rizzio.

Lord Ruthven was both a soldier and a courtier and what he wore on this occasion was suited to either occupation. It consisted of an embroidered buff coat elegant enough for court undress, over which—in case of need—a cuirass could be buckled. Like his father, he was pale, and again like him, he was fated to die young. His features were marked even more than his father's by the peculiar pensiveness by which the augurers of the time claimed to recognize those who were destined to die a violent death.

He combined the polished dignity of a courtier with the inflexibility of a soldier. So, though fully determined to obtain from Mary Stuart, by force if necessary, what he had come to demand in the Regent's name, he nonetheless saluted her respectfully, if somewhat coldly, as he entered. The Queen acknowledged his salutation courteously. The servant then moved the heavy table, which was provided with writing materials, near the empty armchair. At a sign from the two noblemen, he left the room, leaving the Queen and the three emissaries together. The Queen, assuming that the table and the chair were arranged for her, sat down. After a short interval, she herself broke the silence which was more depressing than any words could possibly be.

"My lords," she said, "I wait to learn the purpose of your mission. Is the message that you have brought so terrible that two warriors as renowned as Lord Lindsay and Lord Ruthven should hesitate to deliver it?"

"Madam," Ruthven replied, "I belong to a family which, as you know, never hesitates to perform its duty, however painful that duty may be. Moreover, we hope that your captivity has prepared you to listen to what we have to say on behalf of the Secret Council."

"The Secret Council!" the Queen exclaimed, "by what right does that body, established by me, assume to act without me? But no matter, I await the message. I presume that it is a petition imploring my mercy for those who have dared to arrogate a power which I hold from God alone."

"Madam," returned Ruthven, who seemed to have taken upon himself the office of spokesman while Lindsay remained silent and fingered impatiently the hilt of his long sword, "it is painful for me to undeceive you on this point. It is not your mercy I have come to seek but, on the contrary, to offer you pardon from the Secret Council."

"To me, my lord, to me! Subjects offering pardon to their Queen! Why, the idea is so novel and so astounding that my surprise overcomes my anger. We beg you to continue instead of commanding you to be silent as we ought perhaps to do."

"I will obey you the more willingly, Madam," continued Ruthven imperturbably, "because the pardon is offered only upon certain conditions set forth in these deeds which are intended to re-establish the peacefulness of the realm so grievously compromised by the misdeeds they are intended to correct."

"And are we allowed to read these documents, my lord, or are we expected to sign them blindly, confiding implicitly in the honourable motives of those who present them?"

"No, Madam," Ruthven replied, "the Secret Council expressly wishes that you should have full knowledge of their contents, for you should sign them of your own free will."

"Then read them to me, my lord, for I suppose that that is one of the extraordinary duties you have assumed."

Ruthven took one of the two papers which he was holding and read the following in his usual impassive voice:

"Called at an early age to rule the realm of Scotland we have toiled with the greatest diligence in this, but we have become so weary and discouraged in body and mind that we no longer feel able to bear the burden of affairs of State. Therefore, as Heaven has blessed us with a son to whom we are desirous to ensure, even while we live, the succession to the throne which is his right by birth, we, because of the motherly affection we bear our son, have renounced and demitted, and by these letters of our own free will, renounce and demit the crown and the government of Scotland in favour of our said son that he may succeed us as a native Prince thereof, as much as if we had been removed by natural death and not by our proper and voluntary act. And that this demission of our royal authority may have more full and solemn effect we give, grant and confer full, free and unobstructed power to our faithful cousin Lord Lindsay of Byres and William, Lord Ruthven, to appear in our name before as many of the nobility, clergy and burgesses as may be assembled at Stirling and by these, in our name and on our behalf, publicly and in their presence, do renounce our rights to the crown and government of Scotland.

Signed of our own pleasure, and in witness of the last expression of our royal will, at our castle of Lochleven, this   day of June 1567."

The day of the month had not been inserted.

There was a moment's silence after the reading was concluded.

"Did you hear, Madam?" Ruthven asked.

"Yes," Mary replied, "yes, I heard seditious words which I did not understand, and I thought that my ears which have been for some time accustomed to strange language had deceived me again—and I was led to think that out of respect for your honour, my lords Ruthven and Lindsay."

"Madam," Lindsay broke in impatiently out of his long

silence, "our honour has nothing to do with the opinion of a woman who has been so careless of her own."

"My lord!" Melville ventured to interrupt.

"Let him speak, Melville," said the Queen, "my conscience is protected by a cuirass as well-tempered as the armour in which Lord Lindsay is so prudently dressed although to the shame of justice we no longer have a sword. Continue, my lord," she went on, turning to Ruthven, "is that all my subjects require of me? A date and a signature, ah, that is too little for them to ask. That second document which you have kept until the last doubtless contains something harder to comply with than simply to yield up a crown which is mine by right of inheritance to a child scarcely more than a year old—to throw away my sceptre for a distaff."

"This other document," Ruthven replied, unmoved by the Queen's bitter irony, "is a deed whereby Your Grace confirms the decision of the Secret Council who have appointed your well-beloved brother, the Earl of Murray, Regent of Scotland."

"What do I hear?" Mary cried. "The Secret Council needs my confirmation of an act of so little importance? And my well-beloved brother finds it necessary for his peace of mind that it should be my hand which will bestow upon him a new title in addition to those of Mar and Murray which I have already given him? But all this is most respectful and touching and I should be greatly in the wrong to complain. My lords," she went on, rising from her chair and changing her tone of voice, "return to those who have sent you, and tell them that to such demands Mary Stuart has no reply.

"Beware, Madam," said Ruthven, "and remember that only on these conditions can your pardon be granted."

"And if we refuse this generous pardon what can we then expect?"

"It is not for me to prejudge your cause, Madam. But you are sufficiently conversant with the laws, and particularly the history, of Scotland and England to know that murder and adultery are crimes for which more than one queen has been punished by death."

"And upon what proofs are we accused of such crimes, my lord? Forgive our insistence, which is taking up your valuable time, but we have so much at stake that such a question is surely permissible."

"There is but one, Madam, I admit," Ruthven replied, "but that is irrefutable; it is the precipitate marriage of the victim's widow with the principal assassin, together with the letters handed to us by James Balfour which prove that the guilty persons had committed adultery before they were joined in marriage."

"My lord," the Queen demanded, "have you forgotten a certain meal at a tavern given by this same Bothwell to the very nobles who accuse him today of adultery and murder? Have you forgotten that at the end of the meal, and on the same table as it was eaten, a document was signed urging this same woman to whom you now impute as a crime the speed with which she contracted her latest marriage, to lay aside her widow's weeds for a bridal veil? For if you have forgotten, my lords, it does no credit to your sobriety or your memories. I will undertake to place that paper before your eyes, for I have preserved it, and you may well find among the signatures those of Lindsay of Byres and Ruthven. Oh, noble Lord Herries! Oh, loyal James Melville!" she cried, "you alone were right when you begged me on your knees not to contract that marriage which as we can clearly see today was nothing but a trap set for an ignorant woman by perfidious advisers or disloyal nobles."

"Madam," exclaimed Ruthven, beginning to lose control of himself in spite of his impassivity, while Lindsay was giving more noisy and less equivocal signs of impatience, "Madam, all this discussion is irrelevant to the object of our mission. Let us return to it, and, I beg you, tell us whether your life and honour being assured you will agree to abdicate from the throne of Scotland."

"What guarantee have I that the promises made to me here will be honoured?"

"Our word, Madam," Ruthven proudly replied.

"Your word, my lord, is a poor pledge to offer when you forget your signature so quickly. Have you no other trifle you can add to it which might give me more confidence than I would feel with it alone?"

"Enough, Ruthven, enough!" Lindsay shouted. "Do you not see that for the past hour this woman has responded to our proposals only with insults?"

"Yes, we will go," Ruthven replied, "and blame no one but yourself, Madam, when the thread breaks which holds the sword suspended over your head."

"My lords, my lords, in heaven's name have patience," Melville cried, "and make some allowance for one who is accustomed to command but is today forced to obey."

"You remain with her then," Lindsay said, turning away, "and try to obtain with your smooth tongue what she refuses to our frank and loyal demand. In a quarter of an hour we will return. Let the answer be ready then!"

With this the two peers went out, leaving Melville alone with the Queen.

Their steps could be counted by the clang of Lindsay's huge sword against each stair as they descended.

The moment they were alone Melville threw himself at the Queen's feet.

"Madam," he said, "you have regretted a few moments ago that you had not followed the advice Lord Herries and my brother had given you. Reflect well, Madam, upon the counsel I will give you now, for it is of greater importance than the previous and your regret will be far more bitter if you do not follow it. You cannot tell what may happen, you do not know of what your brother is capable."

"It seems to me," the Queen replied, "that he has given me today sufficient enlightenment on that subject. What more can he do than he has already done? A public trial? I should welcome it. Let them but leave me free to plead my own cause and we shall see what judges will dare to condemn me."

"For that very reason they will be careful to do nothing of the kind, Madam, for it would be the height of folly when they have you safe in this isolated castle guarded by your enemies, and with no witness but God who avenges crimes but does not prevent them. Remember, Madam, what Machiavelli has said 'A king's tomb is never far from his prison'. You come of a family who die young and almost always a violent death. Two of your ancestors died by the sword and one by poison."

"Oh, if death were swift and easy," Mary cried, "I would accept it as an expiation of my faults, for proud though I may be before my enemies I am humble, Melville, when I search my conscience. I am unjustly accused of complicity in Darnley's murder, but I am rightly censured for marrying Bothwell."

"Time flies, Madam, time flies!" Melville exclaimed, glancing at the hour-glass on the table. "They will soon be back and this time you must give them an answer. Listen, Madam, make the best of your plight. You are here with only a single attendant, without friends, protectors or influence. An abdication signed under such circumstances will never appear to your subjects to have been voluntary, but will always be considered to have been torn from you by force. If necessary, Madam, when the day comes to enter your protest, then you will have two witnesses to the duress under which you have acted—Mary Seaton will be one, and the other," he added in an undertone, looking uneasily around, "the other will be Robert Melville."

He had hardly finished speaking when the steps of the absent peers were heard mounting the stairs. They had returned before the allotted time had elapsed. A moment later, the door was thrown open and Ruthven appeared. Lindsay's head could be seen over his shoulder.

"Madam," Ruthven said, "as you see, we have returned. Has Your Grace made up her mind? We want your reply."

"Yes," Lindsay joined in, pushing past Ruthven and approaching the table, "yes, we want a clear, precise and positive answer without any mental reservations."

"You are exacting, my lord," the Queen replied. "You would scarcely have the right to expect so much of me were I on the other side of the loch with my freedom and surrounded by a faithful escort. But within these walls, behind these bars, in the heart of this fortress, although I might say I am signing voluntarily, you would not believe me. But what does it matter, you want my signature and you will have it. Melville, pass me the pen."

"I hope nevertheless," said Ruthven, "that Your Grace does not contemplate entering a protest at some future time against the validity of your signature based on the position in which you now find yourself."

The Queen had already leaned over to write her signature, her hand already on the document, when Ruthven spoke. But the words were no sooner out of his mouth than she rose haughtily to her feet and let the pen drop from her hand.

"My lord," she said, "a few minutes ago your demand was for an abdication pure and simple, and I was on the point of signing it. But if a post-scriptum is to be added to that abdication to the effect that I renounce my rights to the throne of Scotland freely and judging myself unfit to sit thereon, then I will not sign. No, not for the three crowns which have been stolen from me one after the other."

"Beware, Madam," Lindsay shouted, seizing the Queen's wrist with his gauntleted hand and pressing it with all his strength in his anger, "beware, for our patience is at an end, and we may well finish by breaking what will not bend."

The Queen remained standing, and although a violent flush passed like a flame over her face, she neither spoke nor moved. But her eyes looked with such an expression of utter contempt upon the brutal earl that, ashamed at the length to which his rage had carried him, he released her arm and fell back a step. Turning up her sleeve and showing the purple bruises left by Lindsay's gauntlet, Mary said to the emissaries,

"I expected no less, my lords, and nothing now prevents my signing. Yes, I freely abdicate the throne and crown, and here is the proof that I was not coerced."

With these words she seized the pen and rapidly signed both documents, and handed them to Ruthven. With a bow full of dignity, she walked slowly to her bedroom accompanied by Mary Seaton.

Ruthven watched her until she had disappeared.

"It matters not," he said, "she has signed, and although, Lindsay, your method of persuasion is somewhat unusual in diplomacy it is none the less apparently efficacious."

"None of these pleasantries," Lindsay answered. "She is a noble creature, and had I dared I would have fallen at her feet to beg her pardon."

"There is still time," Ruthven sneered, "and in her present situation I fancy that she will not be too hardhearted. Perhaps she has determined to appeal to God's judgment to prove her innocence, and in that case such a champion as you might well put a different face to things."

"That is enough, Ruthven," Lindsay said emphatically, "if I were as convinced of her innocence as I am of her guilt I swear that no man would harm a hair on her head, not even the Regent himself."

"The devil! My lord," Ruthven exclaimed, "I never thought you were so impressionable to a soft voice and tearful eyes. You know the story of Achilles' lance which cured with its rust the wounds its point had made. Do like it, my lord, do like it."

"Ruthven, you are like a cuirass of Milan steel which is three times brighter than a suit of armour made of Glasgow iron and twice as hard. We understand each other, Ruthven, so again I say, enough, enough."

With that Lindsay strode from the room, followed by Ruthven and Melville, the former with head erect and an air of insolent indifference, and the latter sadly and with drooping head not even attempting to disguise the painful impression made upon him by the scene that had taken place.

The Queen did not even leave her room until evening fell, when she resumed her place at the window looking upon the loch. At the accustomed hour she saw the light which was henceforth her only source of hope shining brightly in the little house at Kinross. For a whole long month she had no other consolation than to see it shining there, fixed and faithful, night after night.

Chapter 8

At last, at the end of that month and as she was beginning to despair of ever seeing George Douglas again, Mary opened her window one morning and gave a cry of delight. Mary Seaton ran to her and the Queen, lacking the strength to say anything, pointed to a little boat lying at anchor in the middle of the loch. In it were "Little Douglas" and George indulging in their favourite sport of fishing. The young man had arrived the previous night, but as everyone was accustomed to his unannounced comings and goings the sentinel did not even sound his horn and the Queen was completely unaware that her friend was near her at last.

Three days passed however before she saw the young man except for her first glimpse upon the loch. It is true that George Douglas never, from morning until nightfall, left the spot from which he could see the Queen's windows and, at times, the Queen herself when she pressed her face against the bars. Finally, on the morning of the fourth day, she was awakened by the loud barking of dogs and the blowing of horns. She ran to the window and saw William Douglas embarking with his dogs and whippers-in. He had put aside for a day his duties of gaoler to have some sport in accordance with his rank and birth and was going on a hunting expedition among the woods which covered the lower ridges of the Lomonds and extended to the banks of the loch.

The Queen trembled with joy, for she hoped that Lady Douglas would remain spiteful and that George Douglas would take his brother's place. Her hope was not disappointed. At the usual time, she heard the steps of those who brought her breakfast. The door opened, and George entered, followed by the servants with the dishes. He barely saluted the Queen and she returned his salutation, such as it was, with a disdainful air. But when the servants had carried out their duties and left the room, she exclaimed,

"At last you have returned!"

Signing to her to be silent he went softly to the door to see that none of the servants had stayed behind to spy upon them. Having satisfied himself he came back and said, with great respect,

"Yes, Madam, and thanks be to God, the bearer of good news."

"Oh, tell it to me quickly, for life here is intolerable. You know, do you not, that they came here and forced me to sign an abdication?"

"Yes, Madam, and we know also that your signature was obtained by violence, and now our devotion to Your Majesty has become more absolute, if that were possible."

"But tell me, what have you accomplished?"

"The Seatons and the Hamiltons who, as Your Majesty knows, are your most faithful allies"—here Mary smiled affectionately at Mary Seaton and took her hand—"have already mustered their troops and are ready to move at the first signal. But, as their forces alone are not sufficiently strong to take the field, they will advance directly to Dumbarton, whose governor is friendly, and the situation of that place and its strength will enable them to hold out against the Regent's troops long enough to allow those who remain faithful to you to join us there."

"Yes, yes," said the Queen, "I see the wisdom of the plan and have no fear as to what we shall do when I have regained my liberty. But how are we to escape from here?"

"That, too, is planned, Madam, but its success depends on you summoning all the courage of which you have given great proof."

"If I am only required to display courage and *sang-froid* have no fear. Neither the one nor the other will fail me."

"Here is a file," Douglas continued, handing the tool to Mary Seaton as if he thought it unworthy to touch the Queen's hands. This evening I will bring you ropes with which to make a ladder. You must file through one of the bars of that window which is only twenty feet from the ground. I will, in due course, climb the ladder to test its strength and when the time comes, help you to descend. One of the guards here is in my pay and he will open the gate he guards—and you will be free."

"When will this be?"

"We must wait on two things, Madam. First, until we have assembled at Kinross a sufficient escort to ensure your safety, and secondly, until it is Thomas Warden's turn to stand guard at this isolated gate which we can reach without being seen."

"And how will you know that? Are you remaining in the castle?"

"Hélas! No, Madam. Here I am a useless and perhaps dangerous friend. On the other side of the loch I can help you effectively."

"But how will you know when Warden's turn of duty arrives?"

"The weathercock on the northern tower, instead of turning with the wind like the others, will remain stationary."

"But how am I to know?"

"Everything is provided for. The light which shines every night in the little house at Kinross tells you that your friends are always on the watch. When you wish to know whether the hour of your deliverance is near or still uncertain, place a light in this window and the other will immediately be extinguished. Then put your hand against your heart and count its beats. If you count twenty before the light reappears you will know that nothing yet has been arranged. If you count only to ten it means that the time is near. If you have not time to count beyond five your escape is to be made on the following night. If the light does not reappear at all, it is to be made that very night. In that case the hoot of an owl repeated three times in the courtyard will be the signal for you to let down the ladder."

"Oh, Douglas!" the Queen exclaimed, giving him her hand to kiss, "you alone could have foreseen and provided for everything. Thanks, a hundred times, thanks."

A bright flush spread over the young man's cheeks, but he mastered himself almost immediately. He knelt on one knee and took the hand which Mary offered him and kissed it with so much respect that no one could have seen in the action anything other than the homage of devotion and fidelity. Then, having bowed to the Queen, he left the room before a longer stay should arouse suspicion.

As he promised, Douglas brought a length of rope at dinner-time. It was not long enough, but when night fell Mary Seaton was to let an end hang down from the window and he would attach another piece of sufficient additional length. This was all carried out as arranged and without accident. The following day he left the castle again.

The Queen and her companion lost no time in making the rope ladder and in three days it was finished. That evening, the Queen in her impatience, but more to make sure of the vigilance of her supporters than with any hope that the time for her deliverance was at hand, placed the lamp in the window. Instantly, as Douglas had said, the light in the house went out. The Queen put her hand to her heart and counted twenty-two before the light reappeared; nothing had been definitely decided yet.

For a week she continued to do this without any change in the reply. But on the eighth evening, she counted only to ten and at the eleventh heartbeat the light appeared again. Unable to believe that she was not mistaken and that she had read the meaning of the signal correctly, she took the lamp away and a short time later replaced it in the window. Her unknown signaller at once understood that she wanted the reply repeated. The light in the little house disappeared once more. Once more Mary felt her heartbeat and, fast as it did beat, the star of hope shone again on the horizon before she had counted twelve. There was no further room for doubt, all was arranged.

Mary could not sleep that night and the persistence of her devoted friends moved her to tears. At dawn she questioned her companion again and again to make sure that it had not all been a dream. Every sound that she heard seemed to her to show that the plan upon which her liberty depended had been discovered. When William Douglas came into the room as usual at breakfast time she hardly dared look at him for fear of reading from his expression that all was lost.

That night the Queen again exchanged signals, with the same result. Nothing had changed, the beacon still told her to hope. For five successive nights it continued to indicate that the time was near at hand. On the sixth night, the light reappeared before she had counted to six. Mary leaned against her companion, for between her overjoy and fears she was almost fainting. Her escape was to be effected the following night. She repeated the signal and received the same reply. There could be no further doubt, everything was ready except the prisoner's courage; this failed her for a moment and she would have fallen had not Mary Seaton guided her to a chair. But she soon recovered herself and became stronger and more resolute than ever. She remained at the window until midnight with her eyes fixed on that happy light. At last, Mary Seaton persuaded her to go to bed offering if she could not sleep, to read to her some of Ronsard's poems or chapters from the *Histoires de la mer*. But Mary did not wish to hear any work not concerned with religion and asked her to read from the *Book of Hours*, making the proper responses to the prayers as if she were attending a mass spoken by a priest. Towards daybreak, she dozed off. Mary Seaton, exhausted, at once fell asleep in her chair by the bedside. In the morning she was awakened by a touch on the shoulder. It was the Queen, who was already up.

"Come and look, little one," she said, "come and see what a beautiful day God has given us. How beautiful the world is and what happiness it will be to me to be free once more among the fields and hills. Surely, heaven is on our side."

"Madam," her companion replied, "I would much rather see the weather less beautiful with the promise of a cloudy night. Remember that we must pray for darkness and not for light."

"I agree. It is by that we shall see whether God is really on our side. If the weather remains clear, yes, you are right, I shall believe that He has abandoned us, but if the clouds gather, then little one, will it not be proof of His protection?"

Mary Seaton smiled and nodded her head in approval of her mistress's superstition. The Queen, unable to remain idle while her excitement was so intense, collected the few pieces of jewellery she had kept safe and put them in a box. She also laid out a black dress to help conceal her flight in the darkness. These preparations completed, she resumed her seat at the window and gazed at the house in Kinross which was shut up and lifeless as usual.

Breakfast time arrived. The Queen was so happy that she received William Douglas with more than her customary reserve. It was only with difficulty that she could remain seated during the meal. However, she controlled herself and Douglas left, apparently unconscious of her nervousness.

As soon as the door closed behind him Mary ran to the window again. She thirsted for fresh air, and she gazed hungrily on the vast expanse of country spread out before her. It seemed to her that once she was free again she would never more shut herself up in a palace, but would spend her days wandering through the fields. In the midst of her day-dreams, she felt a strange fear, and then would turn to Mary Seaton seeking new inspiration in her strength. The young woman spoke words of encouragement from a sense of duty rather than from conviction.

Interminable though they seemed to the Queen, the hours

passed. Towards afternoon clouds floated across the sky. Mary joyfully pointed them out to her companion. Dinner time arrived while the two prisoners were watching the drifting clouds. It was again a half-hour of constraint and dissimulation which was the more disagreeable because William Douglas, doubtless to show his appreciation of the Queen's amiability in the morning, felt called upon to make some formal compliments which forced her to take a more active part in the conversation than her preoccupation inclined her to. But Douglas did not seem to notice her absentmindedness and everything passed off as smoothly as it had at breakfast.

When he had gone the Queen once again hurried to the window. The clouds she had seen an hour before had grown heavier and bigger and little sky could be seen. The house at Kinross was still closed and seemed strangely deserted. Night fell and the light shone as usual. Mary gave the customary signal and the light went out. She waited in vain for it to reappear—the attempt at rescue was to be made that night.

She heard eight o'clock strike, then nine and ten when the sentinels were relieved. She heard the steps of the patrol pass under her windows and die away. All was silent again and another half-hour passed. Suddenly an owl hooted three times and the Queen recognized George Douglas's signal. The supreme moment had come, and her strength of character rose up to meet it. She made a sign to Mary Seaton to remove the bar and to tie the rope ladder while she put out the light and went to her bedroom to grope for the box containing her jewels. When she returned, George Douglas was already in the room.

"All is well, Madam," he said, "your friends await you on the other side of the loch, Thomas Warden is on duty at the gate, and God has blessed us with a dark night."

Without replying, the Queen gave him her hand and George Douglas bowed and kissed it. Her hand was shaking and ice-cold.

"Madam, in heaven's name be brave and do not falter now."

"Our Lady of Succour, be thou our helper now," Mary murmured.

"Rather call on the spirit of your royal ancestors, for what you need at this hour is the courage and resolution of a Queen."

"Oh, Douglas, Douglas," cried Mary piteously, "an astrologer once prophesied that I would die a violent death in prison. Has not the hour arrived when this prophecy is to be fulfilled?"

"Perhaps so," Douglas answered, "but how much better to die as a queen than to live in this old castle, deprived of freedom and traduced."

"You are right, but a woman is a creature of impulse. Forgive me." Then after a moment's pause, "Let us go. I am ready."

Douglas at once went to the window, made sure that the ladder was still firmly tied, and then stepped on to it, grasping a bar with one hand and holding out his other hand to the Queen. As resolute now as she was timid a moment before, she stepped on to a stool and had one foot upon the window-ledge when suddenly the cry "Qui vive?" rang out from the foot of the tower. Mary instinctively drew back into the room helped by a push from Douglas who leaned far out to see who had made the challenge which was repeated twice. Meeting no response, this was at once followed by the report of a firearm. At the same instant the sentinel posted on a tower blew his horn while another rang a peal on the alarm-bell. Shouts rang out "To arms! To arms!" and "Treason, treason!" echoed through the castle.

"Yes, yes, treason!" George Douglas shouted, leaping back into the room, "that scoundrel Warden has betrayed us."

He went to Mary who was standing as cold and motionless as a statue.

"Have courage, Madam, have courage. All hope is not lost. You still have one friend in the castle in 'Little Douglas'."

The words were hardly out of his mouth when the door flew open and Lady Douglas and William Douglas appeared on the threshold. They were preceded by servants with torches and armed soldiers. The room was at once filled with people and light.

"Do you believe me now, mother," said William Douglas pointing to his brother, who stood in front of Mary to shield her with his body. "Look!"

For a moment the old lady was speechless, but at last words came to her.

"Speak, George Douglas," she cried, "and clear yourself of the charge which calls in question your honour. Say simply: 'A Douglas has never betrayed his trust', and I will believe you."

"'A Douglas', yes, mother, by birth, but he is no real Douglas," William interposed.

"May God grant my grey hairs the strength to endure such disgrace by one of my sons and the insults of the other. Oh, woman born under a fatal star" she continued, addressing the Queen, "when will you cease to be a tool in the hands of the devil, and the cause of ruin and death to all who come near you? Oh, ancient castle of Lochleven, cursed be the hour when this enchantress crossed its threshold."

"Say not that, mother," George Douglas interrupted, "say rather blessed be the moment which proves that though there are Douglases who have ceased to remember what they owe to their sovereign there are others who have never forgotten."

"Douglas! Douglas!" the Queen murmured, "did I not predict this?"

"And did I not answer, Madam, that it is the duty and honour of every faithful subject of yours to die for you?"

"Then die!" shouted William Douglas, rushing upon his brother with raised sword.

127

George Douglas stepped back, drew his own sword and, with a movement as quick as thought and instinctive with hate, stood on the defensive. But Mary Stuart instantly stood between them.

"Not one step further," she said to the elder brother, "and you, George Douglas, sheathe your sword or make use of it to escape from here against anyone except your brother. I still have need of your life, so guard it well."

"Madam, my life as well as my sword and my honour are at your service, and I obey your command."

With that he darted to the door with a resolution which effectively stopped any intervention.

"Hold back!" he called out, "if you value your lives."

"Stop him!" shouted William Douglas, "seize him dead or alive! Fire on him! Shoot him like a dog!"

Fearing to disobey two or three soldiers made a pretence of following him. A shot or two was heard and a voice called out that George had jumped into the loch.

"He has escaped then," William Douglas cried out furiously.

The Queen breathed freely once more, and the old lady raised her arms appealingly to heaven.

"Yes, yes," muttered William Douglas, "thank God for your son's flight, for it brings lasting disgrace upon the name of Douglas. From now we shall be looked on as accomplices in his treason.

"Have pity on me, William," Lady Douglas moaned, wringing her hands, "in heaven's name have pity on your mother. Can you not see that this has almost killed me?"

Even as she spoke, pale and trembling, she staggered and fell into the arms of the steward and one of the servants.

"I think, my lord," said Mary Seaton, "that your mother needs attention as much as the Queen needs rest. Do you not think that you had better withdraw?"

"Oh, yes," William Douglas retorted, "to give you time to spin new webs and to see what new flies you can entice into them. Very well, do your best, but you will find that it is not easy to deceive William Douglas. Play your game and I will play mine." Then turning to the servants he added, "Leave the room, all of you. And you, mother, come with me."

The servants obeyed and William Douglas went out last, supporting his mother. The Queen heard the outside doors being double-locked behind him.

As soon as Mary was alone and certain that she could be neither seen nor heard all her courage left her. She threw herself into a chair and sobbed as if her heart would break. Indeed, she had needed all the strength she could gather to sustain her in the face of her enemies. But once alone the situation she was in appalled and overwhelmed her. Dethroned, and a prisoner in that impregnable castle, with no friend save a mere child whom she had hardly noticed but who was the last and only connecting link between her past hope and her hopes for the future—what remained to Mary Stuart of her two thrones and her two-fold power? Only her name was left. With that, were she at liberty, she might doubtless have shaken Scotland to its foundations, but imprisoned she would gradually fade from the minds of her supporters and would perhaps, even during her lifetime, be shrouded in oblivion. Such a thought was unendurable to so proud a nature as Mary's whose very being needed air, and light, and sunshine.

Happily, the best-beloved of her four Maries was still at her side, and she, always faithful and tender, hastened to comfort and console her. But it was no easy task and the Queen replied only with sobs and tears. Suddenly Mary Seaton happened to glance through the window near to which she had moved her mistress's chair.

"The light!" she cried, "Madam, the light!"

As she spoke, she raised the Queen in her arms and pointed to the beacon, the never-failing symbol of hope, which shone through the darkness from the house on the hill at Kinross.

There was no possibility of a mistake, for not a star could be seen.

"My God, I thank thee," said the Queen, falling to her knees and raising her hands in prayer. "George Douglas is safe and my friends are still watching."

Then, after a fervent prayer which helped to restore her strength, she went to her bedroom and, worn out by the emotions which had succeeded each other so rapidly, fell into a restless and disturbed sleep. The indefatigable Mary Seaton sat by her bedside until daylight.

As William Douglas had implied, from that day on, the Queen was truly a prisoner. She was not allowed to enter the garden except under the surveillance of two soldiers. The constraint of this arrangement was so irksome to her that she preferred to give up this distraction which in such circumstances became a torture. So she shut herself up in her rooms, finding a certain bitter and proud enjoyment in the very extent of her misery.

Chapter 9

A week after the events just described, as nine o'clock was striking and the Queen and her companion were seated at a table working on a tapestry, a stone was thrown from the garden between the bars in the window. It broke a pane of glass and fell on the floor of the room. The Queen's immediate thought was that it was an accident, or an insult. But Mary Seaton, turning around, saw that it was wrapped in a piece of paper and at once picked it up. The paper proved to be a message from George Douglas:

You ordered me to live, Madam, and I have obeyed you. Your Majesty has seen by the light at Kinross that your servants still watch over you. However, lest suspicion should be raised, the soldiers who were assembled on that fatal night were disbanded at dawn and will only reassemble when a new attempt makes their presence necessary. It would be disastrous to make such an attempt at present when Your Majesty's gaolers are on their guard. Let them take what precautions they will, Madam; let them fall asleep in their imagined security while we, in our devotion, are always watching. Patience and courage!

"Brave and loyal heart!" Mary cried out. "He is more steadfast in our adversity than others were in our prosperity! Yes, I will have patience and courage, and so long as that light continues to shine I will believe I shall yet be free."

The message restored all of the Queen's former courage. She had in "Little Douglas" the means of communicating with George Douglas, for the stone could only have been thrown by the boy. She lost no time in writing a letter in

131

which she bade George Douglas convey her gratitude to all the nobles who had signed the protest and implored them, in the name of the fidelity they had sworn to her, not to let their passion for her cause to grow cold, and promising on her part to await the result of their efforts with the patience and courage they asked of her.

The Queen was not mistaken. Next morning when she went to the window, "Little Douglas" came to play at the foot of the tower. Without looking up, he set to work directly beneath her making a trap to catch birds. Mary looked about her to see if she could be seen. Having made sure that the garden was deserted, she dropped the stone with its letter wrapped around it. At first she thought that she had made a serious mistake—for the boy did not even turn at the sound. And it was some little time, the Queen meanwhile being tortured with anxiety, before he put his hand on the stone as if he were searching for something. Without hurrying and not raising his head he calmly finished what he was doing and then stuffed the stone in a pocket. Thus did he show the Queen, by a self-control beyond his years, how great a confidence might be placed in him.

From that moment Mary took a new hold on hope. But days, weeks and months passed without her situation altering. Winter came and the prisoner saw the snow covering the plains and the mountains. The frozen loch, if only she could be freed, offered a firm path to the shore. In all that time no letter brought her the comforting news that her deliverance would soon be at hand, but every evening the light announced that a friend was watching.

In due course nature awakened. Now and then, stray sunbeams pierced the murky clouds over Scotland. The snow melted, the ice on the loch disappeared, the first buds broke through, and the fields were green once more. Everything came out of its prison, and for Mary it was a bitter sorrow that, for her alone, winter was never-ending.

At last, one night she imagined that the movements of the

light indicated that something new was happening. She had so often questioned the faint, twinkling star, and had so often counted more than twenty, that for a long time, to avoid the agony of disappointment, she had not made any signal. However, she decided to have yet one more try. Without much hope she placed the light in the window. The other light instantly disappeared and was replaced as her heart beat the eleventh time. At the same moment, by a strange coincidence, a stone flew through her window to fall at Mary Seaton's feet. It was, like the first, wrapped in a message from George Douglas. The Queen took it from her, unfolded it and read:

The moment is at hand; your friends are assembled; summon all your courage. Tomorrow night at eleven hang a rope from your window and pull up the package which will be tied to it.

The rope, left over after making the ladder which the guards carried away on the night of the abortive attempt at escape, was still in the Queen's room. Next night at the hour named the prisoners took the lamp to the bedroom so that their movements might not be detected. Mary Seaton went to the window and lowered the rope. In a moment she could feel that something was being attached to it. She drew it up and found that the package was too big to be taken through the bars. The Queen came to her help and they untied the package; the articles in it came easily between the bars one by one. They took them all into the bedroom and having locked themselves in began their inventory. The contents proved to be two complete sets of a manservant's distinctive dress of the Clan Douglas. The Queen could make nothing of it at first, but finally she found a letter fastened to the collar of one of the two doublets. Eager to learn the answer to the riddle she quickly opened it and read:

Only sheer audacity will enable Your Majesty to regain your liberty. We therefore beg you to read this message carefully and if you agree to adopt the proposed plan, follow the instructions given. The castle keys never leave the old steward's belt during the day. When curfew has been sounded and he has made his last round to make sure that all doors and gates are firmly secured he hands them to William Douglas who, if he passes the night on guard, attaches them to his sword-belt, but if he is not, puts them under his pillow. For the past five months Little Douglas has been allowed to watch the work in the armourer's forge at the castle and has managed in doing this to fashion a set of keys sufficiently like the genuine ones to deceive William Douglas if the substitution can be carried out. Yesterday "Little Douglas" finished the last one.

At the first favourable opportunity, and Your Majesty will know when it has arrived by questioning the light every night without fail, the boy will substitute the false keys for the genuine ones, will enter Your Majesty's rooms where he will find you and Mary Seaton dressed in your male costumes and will conduct you by the route which will offer the best chance of escape. A boat will await you.

Until that time arrives you both must wear these costumes nightly from nine until twelve, not only to accustom yourselves to them but also to give them the appearance of having been worn for some time. It is also possible that your young guide may come for you unexpectedly, having had no time to warn you in advance. It is of the utmost importance that you should be found prepared for flight.

The clothes should fit you both perfectly as Mary Fleming and Mary Livingston, who are much of the same figure, were measured for them.

We cannot impress too strongly on Your Majesty the necessity of calling to your aid at this supreme crisis the coolness and courage which you have shown so often at other times.

The two prisoners were astounded by the daring of the plan and, at first, they gazed at each other in consternation, for it seemed to them that success was impossible. Nevertheless, they tried on their disguises and, as George Douglas had said, found that the clothes did, indeed, fit them perfectly.

Obedient to the instructions the Queen each night questioned the light. For a whole tedious month she and Mary Seaton never failed to get dressed in the clothes sent to them. Thus they became so accustomed to them that they were as much at home in them as in their own clothes.

At last, on 2 May 1568, the Queen was awakened by the blowing of a horn. Anxious to know what it was all about she put on a dressing-gown and ran to the window where she was soon joined by Mary Seaton. A large number of horsemen were standing on the shore of the loch with the Douglas banner, and three boats were being rowed to the shore to bring the new arrivals to the castle.

This event was an alarming one for the Queen. The slightest change in the regular routine of the castle was to be dreaded as it might overthrow all their carefully laid plans. Her apprehensions redoubled as the boats approached the island—for she saw in the largest one Lord Douglas, the husband of Lady Douglas and father of William and George. The old nobleman, who was Warden of the Northern Marches, had come to visit his old home for the first time in three years. This was a great event at Lochleven. A few minutes after the arrival of the boats Mary heard the step of the steward climbing the stairs. He came to tell the Queen of his master's arrival and, as the return of Lord Douglas was to be the occasion of a fête, to invite her to the banquet which was to form part of the celebrations. The Queen refused, partly from instinct, and partly because such an invitation was repugnant to her.

All day long the bell and the horn were being sounded. Lord Douglas, like a true feudal chieftain, travelled with the retinue of a prince. New faces of soldiers, servants, valets, and grooms passed continually back and forth under the Queen's windows. Each wore a livery similar to that which she and Mary Seaton had received.

Mary impatiently waited for nightfall. The previous night she had questioned the light. It had replied as usual by reappearing at the eleventh or twelfth heartbeat, telling her that the time of escape was near. But she was greatly alarmed lest Lord Douglas's arrival had upset the plans and that the light when it next appeared would announce a postponement. So, the instant she saw the distant gleam she signalled it; the other immediately disappeared. Mary, in an agony of suspense, began to count. Her agitation increased when she had counted beyond fifteen. She stopped counting and stood, utterly discouraged, gazing mechanically at the spot where the light had shone. But to her amazement it failed to reappear at all. After half an hour had passed all was still dark. She then repeated the signal, but there was no reply. The escape was to be that same night.

They had so little expected that anything would be attempted then that they had not changed into the clothes provided. They rushed into the Queen's room, barricaded the door, and began to change. Their hurried toilette was barely completed when they heard a key turn in the lock of the outer door and they at once put out their lamp. Soft steps approached and the two women leaned on each other for they were both near fainting. There was a gentle knock on their door. The Queen asked who was there and "Little Douglas's" voice replied with the first two lines of an old ballad:
"Douglas, Douglas,
Tender and true."

Mary immediately opened the door for it was the countersign agreed upon earlier with George Douglas. The boy had no light, but he stretched out his hand until it touched the Queen's. By the faint light of the stars, she saw him kneel and then she felt his lips touch her fingers.

"Is Your Majesty ready to follow me?" he asked in a whisper as he stood up once more.

"Yes, my child, but is it to be tonight?"

"With Your Majesty's permission, yes."

"Everything is ready then?"

"Everything."

"What have we to do?

"Follow me wherever I go."

"Oh, merciful God, have pity on us." She repeated a short prayer under her breath while Mary Seaton went and fetched the box containing the jewels.

"Now I am ready," the Queen said, "and you, little one?"

"I am ready also," her attendant answered.

"Come then," said the boy.

The prisoners followed him, the Queen walking first. The boy carefully closed the door so that no guard on his rounds would notice anything and then began descending the spiral staircase. When they were halfway down the noise of the festivities reached their ears, a mixture of loud laughter, the confused hum of voices, and the clinking of glasses. The Queen put a hand on her young guide's shoulder.

"Where are you leading us?" she asked in dismay.

"Out of the castle."

"But must we pass through the great hall?"

"Certainly. That is exactly what George foresaw and provided for. Among the servants all dressed in the same livery, no one will recognize you."

"Oh, my God, my God," murmured the Queen leaning against the wall for support.

"Have courage, Madam," whispered Mary Seaton, "or we are lost."

"You are right," the Queen answered, "let us go on."

They continued down the stairs, still behind their guide. At the foot of the stairs he stopped and handed the Queen a stone jug filled with wine.

"Put this on your right shoulder, Madam. It will hide

your face from those at the table, and carrying something you will be less likely to cause suspicion. You, Mary Seaton, hand me the box and put this basket of bread on your head. Now, are you ready and do you feel able to go on?"

"Yes," the two women answered simultaneously.

A few steps further on they found themselves in a sort of ante-room leading to the great hall. Several servants were there occupied in various ways, but no one paid any attention to them and the Queen was more reassured. In any case it was too late to turn back as "Little Douglas" was now entering the hall.

The guests, seated on both sides of a long table and placed according to their rank, had reached the dessert stage—the most convivial moment of the whole banquet. But the hall was so vast that the lamps and candles by which it was lighted, numerous as they were, left the two sides, where fifteen to twenty servants were coming and going in a kind of semi-darkness, very much in the favour of the fugitives. The Queen and Mary Seaton mingled with the servants who were too busy to take any notice of them. Without once stopping, without losing courage, without looking back, they crossed the whole length of the hall and passed through a door at the other end into an ante-room similar to the one they had come into at the foot of the stairs. There the Queen put down her jug and Mary Seaton her basket and, still under the boy's guidance, they entered a corridor at the end of which they found themselves in a courtyard. A patrol was passing at the moment but he paid no attention to them.

They followed their guide towards the garden and here he was forced to spend some time finding the right key to open the gate. It was a moment of near panic. At last the key turned in the lock and the gate opened. The two women rushed into the garden while the boy locked the gate behind them.

Two-thirds of the way across he raised his hand and signed to them to stop. He laid the box and the keys on the ground, cupped his hands to his mouth, and three times imitated the hooting of an owl with such perfection that it was impossible to believe a human voice had made the sounds. Then he picked up the box and the keys and continued on tip-toe, listening intently as he went. When they were near the wall, they halted again and after a moment's suspense and anxiety, they heard a groan and the sound of a body falling. Some few seconds later there was the answering owl-hoot signal.

"It is done," "Little Douglas" coolly remarked, "now let us be on our way."

"What is done," the Queen asked, "and what was that groan we heard?"

"There was a sentinel at the gate which opens on to the loch, but he is no longer there."

The Queen felt her blood run cold, for she now understood it all. Some poor wretch had been killed because of her. She leaned trembling on Mary Seaton who was herself almost at the end of her strength. Meanwhile "Little Douglas" was trying his keys, and the second one opened the gate.

"The Queen?" whispered a man's voice from the other side of the wall.

"She is behind me," the boy answered.

George Douglas darted into the garden and, taking the Queen's arm in one hand and Mary Seaton's in the other, hurried them to the shore of the loch. As she passed through the gate Mary could not help but glance uneasily around her, and she thought she saw a shapeless mass huddled at the foot of the wall. A shudder ran through her.

"Have no pity for him," George Douglas said in an undertone, "for it is heaven's justice. That man was the scoundrel, Warden, who betrayed us."

"Hélas," said the Queen, "guilty though he may have been he died nonetheless because of me."

"When your safety is in question, Madam, can we haggle over the shedding of worthless blood? But quiet. This way, follow me this way. Let us keep along the shadow of the wall. The boat is twenty feet away, and then we are safe."

With that he drew the fugitives along more swiftly than before and all four reached the water's edge without being seen. A small boat was lying awaiting them. When they saw the four coming, the four oarsmen who were lying in the bottom rose to their feet and one of them leaped ashore and drew the little craft up so that the Queen and her companion could step aboard. George Douglas seated them at the bow and the boy took his place at the tiller. George, with one foot on the shore, gave a vigorous push which sent the boat well out on to the loch.

"Now," he said, "we are truly out of danger, for they might as well chase a swallow on Solway Firth as try to overtake us. Row, men, row. Never mind who hears us. All we want is speed."

"Who goes there?" a voice called out from one of the castle towers.

"Row, row," George Douglas cried, and placed himself in front of the Queen.

"A boat, a boat!" the same voice cried. And then seeing that the little craft continued its course—"Treason! Treason! To arms!"

An instant later a flash lit up the loch, followed by a report, and a ball whistled over their heads. The Queen shrieked, but she was in no danger with George Douglas shielding her. The alarm bell was now ringing madly and lights could be seen moving swiftly from window to window in the castle.

"Courage," cried George Douglas, "and row as if your lives hung on every stroke. The skiff may be after us in five minutes."

"They will not come as soon as you think," "Little Douglas" interrupted, "for I locked everything behind me. It will be a long time before the keys I left behind will do any unlocking. These," he added, holding up the bunch he had so adroitly gained possession of, "I will present to Kelpie, the spirit of the loch, and appoint him porter of the castle."

The report from a small piece of artillery was his answer.

But the night was so dark that it was impossible to aim accurately at so great a distance and the shot ricocheted some fifty feet away from the boat, its echo ringing from shore to shore. George Douglas then drew a pistol from his belt and, with a word of warning to his companions, fired into the air. This was not a show of bravado by way of reply to the castle but a signal to the troop of faithful friends waiting on the bank of the loch—that the Queen was safe. At once shouts of joy were heard, despite the fact that Kinross village was only a short distance away. The young helmsman steered in the direction of the voices and ran the boat ashore. George Douglas gave his hand to the Queen who sprang lightly to the bank where she fell on her knees and gave thanks to God for her deliverance.

Rising, she found herself surrounded by her most trusted adherents: Hamilton, Herries and Seaton, Mary's father. Wild with joy the Queen held out her hands to them, stammering her thanks in broken words which expressed more eloquently than the most formal phrases her delight and gratitude. Suddenly, turning round, she saw George Douglas standing sadly aloof and she instantly went to him and took his hand.

"My lords," she said, leading him forward and pointing to "Little Douglas", "here are my two liberators to whom, as long as I live, I shall owe a debt of gratitude which I can never hope to repay."

"Madam," replied George Douglas, "each of us has done simply what we had to do, and he who has risked most is the happiest. But, if Your Majesty is well-advised, she will waste no time in useless words."

"Douglas is right," said Seaton, "To horse! To horse!"

Four couriers were at once dispatched in different directions to announce the Queen's successful escape to her supporters. With all her old grace she sprang upon the back of a horse which had been lead forward for her, and the little troop consisting of about twenty people escorted her. They made a detour to avoid the village of Kinross, which was sure to have been wakened by the firing from the castle, and rode rapidly for Seaton's castle where there was a large enough garrison to protect her from any sudden attack.

The Queen stayed in the saddle all night, Douglas riding on one side and Seaton on the other. At daybreak they halted at the gate of the castle of West-Niddrie in West Lothian, belonging to Seaton. Douglas quickly alighted to offer his hand to the Queen, but Seaton claimed this privilege as host. Mary consoled Douglas with a smile and entered the castle.

"Madam," Seaton said, conducting her to the room which had awaited her coming for nine months, "you must be in urgent need of rest after the fatigue and excitement of the past twenty-four hours. Sleep peacefully and be alarmed by nothing. Any noise which you may hear will be caused by the arrival of reinforcements we are awaiting. As for your enemies, Your Majesty has nothing to fear while you are under a Seaton's roof."

The Queen again thanked her rescuers, again gave her hand to George Douglas to kiss, kissed "Little Douglas" on the forehead, and told him that for the future he would be her personal page. Then, following the advice that had been given, she withdrew to her bedroom where Mary Seaton claimed the exclusive privilege of still performing the duties which had been hers during their eleven months of captivity.

When she reopened her eyes Mary Stuart thought for a moment that she had been dreaming one of those dreams which are so painful to a prisoner who awakens to find the bolts still in place on the door and the windows barred. Hardly believing the evidence of her eyes she ran half-clothed to the window. The courtyard was filled with soldiers, all of them friends who had flocked to the castle upon learning of her escape. She recognized the banners of her faithful followers: the Seatons, Arbroaths, Herries and Hamiltons. She was no sooner seen at the window than all these banners were lowered before her, and shouts of "Long live Mary of Scotland! Long live our Queen!" greeted her.

Disregarding momentarily her state of undress, she bowed and smiled, her eyes brimming with tears—but the tears were tears of joy. Suddenly she became aware of her undress and quickly came away from the window blushing with confusion and shame that she had let her emotion lead her to such forgetfulness. She was worried by the fact that she had escaped from Lochleven in man's clothing and had had no opportunity to collect her own clothes. Obviously, she could not remain dressed as a manservant and spoke of her dilemma to Mary Seaton who replied by opening the wardrobe in the Queen's bedroom. It was filled not only with dresses which, like the livery, had been made to fit Mary Fleming but also with all the accessories for a woman's toilet. The Queen was amazed; it seemed as if she had entered an enchanted castle.

"Little one," she said, looking through the dresses the materials for which had been selected with excellent taste, "I knew your father to be a brave and loyal man, but I did not think him to be a connoisseur in matters of dress. We will make him master of our wardrobe."

"Ah, Madam," Mary Seaton smilingly replied, "you are mistaken. My father has seen to the polishing of every cuirass, the sharpening of every sword, the unfurling of every banner to be found in the castle, but although he is only too ready to die for you, it would never have occurred to him to offer anything more than a roof over your head and his cloak to cover you. It was George Douglas who foresaw and prepared everything, everything including Rosabelle your favourite hack, which is waiting impatiently in the stable for the moment you will make your triumphal entry into Edinburgh on her back."

"But how did he recover her for me? I had thought that in the division of all my property Rosabelle had been handed to the beautiful Alice, my brother's favourite mistress."

"And so she was, and knowing the animal's value, Alice kept her under lock and key and guarded by a small army of grooms. But Douglas can perform miracles. As I have told you Rosabelle is here."

"The noble Douglas," murmured the Queen, with tears in her eyes. "And yet," she added, as if speaking to herself, "yours is a devotion which cannot be repaid. Others can be content with titles, positions or riches. But what are such things to Douglas."

"Come, Madam," said her companion, "God assumes the obligations of kings and He will reward Douglas. And I must remind you," she added with a smile, "that dinner awaits you. And I hope you do not intend to affront my father as you did Lord Douglas yesterday by refusing to join in the festivities to celebrate your safe return."

"It was fortunate that I did. But let us be finished with gloomy thoughts, little one. We will consider when we are really Queen again what we can do for Douglas."

The Queen dressed and went downstairs. The principal nobles of her party who had already arrived awaited her in the castle's great hall. Her entrance was greeted with tumultuous enthusiasm and she took her place at table with Seaton on her right, George Douglas on her left, and "Little Douglas" behind her chair filling, for the first time, his office of page.

The next morning Mary was wakened by the sounding of trumpets and horns. It had been agreed the previous evening that they should leave that day for Hamilton where further reinforcements awaited them. She was dressed in an elegant costume and appeared among her protectors mounted on Rosabelle. The shouts of joy redoubled, for everyone admired her loveliness, her grace, and her spirit. Mary Stuart was herself again, and she felt her grip tighten upon that power of fascination which she had always exercised over all who came near her. Everyone was in high spirits, and perhaps the happiest of all was "Little Douglas" who for the first time in his life wore fine clothes and rode a beautiful horse.

Two or three thousand men awaited the Queen at Hamilton where she arrived the same evening. During the night which followed her arrival her force was increased to six thousand.

On the second of May, she was a prisoner with no other friend in her prison except a young boy, and no other means of communication with her adherents than the flickering and uncertain light of a lamp. Three days later, between Sunday and Wednesday, she was not only free, but at the head of a powerful alliance which numbered among its leaders nine earls, eight barons, nine bishops, as well as a great many knights and gentlemen from the most renowned in Scotland for gallantry.

The advice of the most prudent of those in attendance on the Queen was to withdraw to Dumbarton Castle which was practically impregnable. By so doing her partisans however far away and scattered they might be would gain time to rally round her standard. In accordance with that advice the command of the troops escorting her to Dumbarton was entrusted to the Earl of Argyle. On the eleventh of May, she set out with an army of about ten thousand men.

Chapter 10

Murray was at Glasgow when he learned of the Queen's escape, and the town being strongly fortified he decided to remain there. He summoned the bravest and most devoted of his faction to join him—Kirkcaldy of Grange, Morton, Lindsay of Byres, Douglas and William Douglas responded promptly, and six thousand of the best troops of the kingdom assembled around him. Ruthven was raising levies in Berwick and Angus with which he was to join them.

At daybreak on the thirteenth of May, Morton occupied the village of Langside through which the Queen had to pass on her way to Dumbarton. News of this move reached her when the armies were about nine miles apart. Remembering her experience at Carberry Hill, which resulted in her separation from Bothwell and bringing her to Edinburgh, her first impulse was to try to avoid a battle. She was supported by George Douglas who had stayed at her side clad in a plain suit of armour.

"Avoid a battle!" Seaton cried, addressing Douglas as if the idea had been his and not daring to reply to his sovereign directly. "We might do that if we were one against ten, but most certainly not when we are three against two. You give strange advice, young man," he continued scornfully, "and you seem to forget that you are a Douglas and are speaking to a Seaton."

"My lord," George Douglas calmly replied, "if we were risking the lives of only the Seatons and the Douglases you would find me as willing to fight as yourself whether we were one against ten or three against two. But we are now responsible for a life which is more precious to Scotland than those of all the Seatons and the Douglases. My advice still is that we should avoid a battle."

"Let us fight! Let us fight!" All the leaders cried with one voice.

"You hear, Madam?" Seaton said to Mary. "They are unanimous, and I believe to decide otherwise would be dangerous. There is an old Scottish proverb, Madam, which says that courage is the greatest prudence."

"But you heard it said, did you not," the Queen replied, "that the Regent's troops hold a strong position?"

"The greyhound pursues the hare over the hill as well as over the plain," was Seaton's answer. "However strong his position we will dislodge him."

"As you think best, my lords. It shall never be said that Mary Stuart ordered her friends to sheathe the swords which they had drawn in her defence." Then turning to Douglas she said, "George Douglas, choose a bodyguard of twenty men and take command of it. You must not leave my side."

Douglas bowed in obedience, picked twenty of the bravest men, placed the Queen in their centre and put himself at their head. The march was then resumed. In about two hours the vanguard came in sight of the enemy. A halt was made until the rest of the army caught up with them.

The Queen's forces were then abreast of the city of Glasgow. The higher land before them was already occupied by a considerable force flying, as did Mary's army, the royal standard of Scotland. On the other side, and upon the the opposite slopes of the hill, lay the village of Langside surrounded by gardens. The road leading there followed the natural lie of the land and was so narrow at one point that two men could barely walk abreast. Further on it plunged into a narrow gorge. When it emerged on the other side the road branched, one route leading up the hill to Langside and the other turning off to Glasgow.

When the Earl of Argyle saw how the land lay he understood immediately the importance of gaining possession of the village. Turning to Seaton he ordered him to leave at the gallop and to gain possession of it from Morton. Seaton at once gathered his men together, but while they were collecting around his banner, Arbroath drew his sword and rode up to Argyle.

"My lord," he said, "you wrong me by sending Seaton to seize this position. As commander of the vanguard that honour belongs to me, and I trust no one will dispute my right."

"The order to seize that position was given to me and it is I who will execute it," Seaton shouted.

"That may be so," replied Arbroath, "but not in advance of me."

"In advance of you and all the Hamiltons," Seaton cried, and galloped off down the narrow road shouting: "Saint Bennet! Forward!"

"Follow me, my men," from Arbroath, dashing away in the same direction. "Forward, for God and the Queen!"

Both bodies of troops followed their chieftains in a disorderly array and crowded along the narrow path. There a struggle began between friends who should have shown a united front against the common enemy. At last they crowded through to the gorge and left behind them the bodies of many who were stifled in the crush or killed in scuffles between the clans. But Seaton and Arbroath, during this senseless struggle, had lost valuable time and the detachment sent by Murray had already joined in possession of the village. Then Argyle, in command of the remaining main body of the Queen's army, ordered a rearguard of two thousand men to hold their present position and await further orders before joining in the battle. But the officer to whom he entrusted this command either misunderstood his orders or wished to distinguish himself in the Queen's eyes. For Argyle had no sooner disappeared into the gorge, at the further end of which Kirkcaldy of Grange and Morton were engaged in combat with Arbroath and Seaton, than he too set off at full speed, disregarding the Queen's cries and leaving her with no other guard than the little escort of twenty men chosen by Douglas. The latter heaved a sigh which the Queen overheard.

"Hélas," she said, "I am no soldier, but it seems to me that the battle is badly begun."

"What can be expected?" Douglas replied. "From the highest to the lowest we are the victims of a sort of light-headedness and all these men today are behaving like fools or children."

"Victory! Victory!" The Queen suddenly called out. "Look, the enemy is retreating. I can see the banners of Seaton and Arbroath waving among the first houses of the village. Oh, my gallant lords!" she cried, clapping her hands. "Victory! Victory!"

But her enthusiasm was quickly quenched as she saw a hostile force advancing to attack on the flank.

"As long as there is none but cavalry in the advance there is little to worry about," George Douglas said. "And besides Argyle will come up in time in support."

"Look George," said "Little Douglas", pointing to the enemy who were galloping towards the village.

"What is it?"

"Each horseman has an arquebusier on his crupper and the force is twice as strong as it looks."

"That is indeed true. You have sharp eyes. Someone must go at once to warn Argyle."

"Let me go," the boy said. "I saw them first and have the right to bring the warning."

"Go then," said Douglas, "and God be with you."

The boy flew off like an arrow, not hearing, or pretending not to hear, the Queen call him back. They watched him travel down the narrow road and saw him plunge into the gorge just at the moment Argyle emerged from the other side to reinforce Seaton and Arbroath. Meanwhile, the infantry of the enemy's detachment had scattered along the side of the gorge where horses could not go.

"He will arrive too late," Douglas said, "and even should he get there in time the warning will be useless. Fools, fools that we are. This is how we have lost all our battles."

"Is the day then lost?" Mary asked, with colourless cheeks.

"No, Madam, no, not yet, thank God. But because of too great haste it has been started badly."

"And what of that young boy?"

"He is now having his first taste of battle, and unless I am very mistaken he should be at the spot where the arque-busiers are firing."

"Poor boy! If anything happens to him I will never forgive myself."

"Hélas, Madam, I am greatly afraid that his first battle will be his last and that now it is all over with him, for this is his horse returning riderless."

"Oh, my God, my God!" the Queen cried. "Am I destined to bring death to all who love me!"

George Douglas was not wrong, for it was "Little Douglas's" horse, riderless, and covered in blood.

"Madam," Douglas said, "we are badly placed here. Let us ride to the top of that hill to Crookstane Castle. From there we can see the whole field of battle."

"No, not there, not there," the Queen almost shrieked, "it was in that castle that I passed the first days of my marriage to Darnley. It would bring me bad luck."

"Very well then, under that yew there," Douglas answered, pointing to another hill near the first. "It is important we should lose no detail of the battle. Your Majesty's fate may well depend upon a badly judged manoeuvre or a lost opportunity."

"Lead me there, then, for I can no longer see my way, and every discharge of those terrible guns echoes to the bottom of my heart."

Although the hill which they climbed was so situated as to command a view of the whole field of battle, the continual firing of guns produced so thick a cloud of smoke that it was impossible to distinguish anything save shapeless, struggling masses. At last, when the conflict had lasted an hour, fleeing men could be seen emerging from the smoke and scattering in all directions pursued by the victors. But at that distance it was hopeless to try and make out who had won or lost the day. Nor did the standards help, for both of the contending armies carried banners bearing the arms of Scotland.

Suddenly they saw the last of the reserve of Murray's army descending the hill from the direction of Glasgow to join in the fray—but this manoeuvre might as well be to support the retreat of his troops as to carry out the final defeat of the Queen's partisans. However, it was not long before all doubt was removed, for the reserves charged the fugitives with the result that there was renewed confusion among them.

The Queen's army was vanquished.

And as they became convinced that this was so, three or four horsemen appeared out of the gorge and galloped towards them. Douglas recognized them as enemies.

"Fly, Madam," he shouted, "fly at once for they will soon be followed by others. Cover as much distance as possible while I hold them back. And you men," turning to her escort, "die to the last man rather than let your Queen be taken."

"Douglas! Douglas!" the Queen called out.

But Douglas had already ridden away at full speed. As he was mounted on a magnificent horse he crossed the intervening space like lightning to reach the narrow path before his adversaries. There he stopped, put his lance at the ready, and coolly awaited the onset—one man against five.

As for the Queen, she could not make up her mind to fly but remained petrified at the same place staring at the combat taking place less than five hundred yards from her. She suddenly noticed that one of George Douglas's opponents bore in the centre of his shield a bleeding heart, the Douglas

crest. With lowered head and a cry of sorrow she murmured:
"Douglas against Douglas, brother against brother. It needed
only this."

"Madam! Madam!" her escort called out. "There is not a
moment to lose. The young Douglas cannot hold out against
five. Let us flee!"

Two of them seized the Queen's bridle on either side and
they then set off at a gallop just as George Douglas, after
killing two of his enemies and wounding a third, was himself
killed, his heart pierced by a lance. The Queen groaned
as she glanced back and saw him fall. Then, as if he alone
had detained her and now that he was dead she had no
further interest in anything, she gave Rosabelle her head. As
she and her escort were splendidly mounted, the battlefield
was soon left far behind.

She rode sixty miles without stopping, without ceasing to
weep. At last, after riding across Renfrewshire and Ayrshire,
she reached Dundrennan Abbey in Galloway. Being certain
that, for a time at least, she was out of danger, she ordered a
halt. The prior came to the gate and received her respectfully.

"I bring you misfortune and sorrow, Father," she said,
dismounting.

"You are welcome," the prior responded, "since it is part
of my duty to console those who have suffered misfortune
and are sad."

The Queen handed over Rosabelle to one of the escort.
Supported by Mary Seaton, who had never left her side, and
Herries, who had joined her on the road, she entered the
priory. Herries did not try to conceal from her the gravity of
her situation. The battle had resulted in total defeat, and with
the defeat, all hope of her reascending the throne was swept
away—for the time being at least. She was left with three
alternatives—she could return to France, she could go to
Spain, or go to England. On Herries' advice, which fell in
with her own wishes, she decided upon England. That same
night she wrote Elizabeth a double letter, in prose and in verse:

My dear sister,

I have often prayed you to receive my storm-tossed
ship in your harbour during the tempest. If she now finds
safe haven there I will cast anchor there for my remaining days. Otherwise the poor craft is in God's care, but
she is well-caulked and prepared to face all the storms
that blow. I have always proceeded fairly with you, and
do still. Do not take it in bad part that I write thus for I
do not mistrust you, as you can see, for I put my utmost
faith in your friendship.

These verses accompanied the letter:

A single thought there is which comforts and torments
me and, without ceasing, changes sweet to bitter in my
heart as hope and doubt alternately oppress me, for
peace and rest have long flown away.

So, dear sister, if this card pursues the keen desire
by which I am oppressed to see you, it is because I abide
in sorrow and distress unless a sweet result should not
soon ensue.

I have seen my barque forced to anchor in the deep
when close to port, and storm succeed fair weather.

Thus am I oppressed by grief and fear, not for your
sake but because Fortune so often breaks the strongest
rope and sail.

Elizabeth trembled with joy on the receipt of the letter.
For the past eight years her hatred of Mary Stuart had
increased daily, and she had constantly followed the events
in Mary's life—just as the wolf follows the gazelle. At last
the gazelle had come of her own free will into the wolf's
lair. It was more than Elizabeth had dared to hope. She at
once sent a command to the Lord Lieutenant of Cumberland
to tell Mary that she was willing to receive her in her kingdom. So, one morning, there was heard the blare of a trumpet
on the shore; it announced the arrival of Queen Elizabeth's
envoy to Queen Mary.

The most urgent appeals were then made to the fugitive

not to trust so powerful a rival, but the poor, dethroned Queen had perfect confidence in her "good sister" and believed that she would enjoy at Elizabeth's court the position due to her rank and misfortunes. So in spite of all that was said she persisted in her determination.

Mary, therefore, set out with her little retinue. When they reached the shore of Solway Firth they were met by a gentleman named Lowther who received the Queen with the greatest deference, but told her that he could allow only three of her women to accompany her. Mary Seaton immediately claimed the privilege of being one of them. The Queen held out her hand to her and said,

"Hélas, little one, it should be another's turn now, for you have already suffered enough for me and with me."

But Mary Seaton, unable to reply, clung to her hand and shook her head as if to say that nothing in the world could separate her from her mistress.

Then all those who had accompanied the Queen renewed their entreaties to her not to persist in her fatal determination. When she was even a third of the way along the plank leading to the boat, the prior of Dundrennan, who had given her such touching hospitality when it was a most dangerous thing for him to do, waded into the water to his knees trying to restrain her. But it was all to no purpose. The Queen's resolution was not to be shaken. It was then that Lowther came forward.

"Madam," he said, "accept my regrets once more that I am unable to extend a cordial welcome in England to all who would wish to follow you there, but our Queen has given strict commands on the matter and it is my duty to carry them out. And may I observe to Your Majesty that the tide is now favourable for us?"

"Strict commands!" cried the prior. "Do you hear Madam? Oh, you are lost if you leave this shore. Turn back while there is still time! Return, Madam, in heaven's name! Help, gentlemen, help!" he shouted, turning towards

Herries and the other men in Mary's suite. "Do not allow your Queen to abandon you. Detain her by force if need be even though you have to struggle with her as well as the English."

"What is the meaning of this violence, priest?" Lowther asked. "I am here because of the express request of your Queen. But she is free to return with you and there need be no question of force. Madam," he continued, turning to the Queen, "is it your desire to follow me into England of your own free will? Tell me, I entreat you, for it is most important that the whole world should know that you accompanied me willingly."

"Sir," Mary answered, "I beg your pardon on behalf of this worthy servant of God and his Queen for any offence that he has given you. I leave Scotland of my own free will and place myself in your hands fully confident that I shall be free to remain in England with my royal sister or to return to my kinsfolk in France. Your blessing, Father," she went on, looking at the prior, "and may God protect you."

"Hélas, hélas," the prior murmured, "it is not we who have need of God's protection, but you, my daughter. May a poor priest's blessing ward from your royal head the misfortunes which I foresee. Go, and may it be with you as God in his wisdom and mercy has decreed."

Thereupon the Queen gave her hand to Lowther who led her aboard the boat, Mary Seaton and only two other women attendants followed. The sails were hoisted at once and the little craft moved swiftly away from the shores of Galloway towards Cumberland. As long as it was in sight Mary's friends remained at the water's edge waving farewell to their Queen, who stood at the stern herself waving her handkerchief in return. At last the boat faded from sight, and they made no further attempt to hide their tears and sadness. Their grief was fully justified, for the good prior's presentiments came true and none of them ever saw Mary Stuart again.

When she landed on English soil the Queen of Scotland

was met by messengers from Elizabeth who were instructed to express to her their Queen's profound regret at her inability either to admit Mary to her presence or to give her the affectionate welcome which her heart dictated. But it was essential, they said, that she should prove her innocence of all complicity in Darnley's death as his family, being subjects of Queen Elizabeth, were entitled to her protection and claimed justice from her.

Mary was so blind that she failed to see the trap and at once offered to prove her innocence to the satisfaction of her sister Elizabeth. But no sooner did the English queen receive her letter than she changed from arbiter to judge, appointed commissioners to hear the parties, and summoned Murray to appear as his sister's accuser.

Chapter 11

Murray was fully aware of Elizabeth's secret intentions with regard to her rival and did not hesitate for a moment. He came to England with the casket containing the three letters, the verses and other documents, proving that not only had Mary been Bothwell's mistress during Darnley's lifetime but that she had also showed her knowledge of the manner of the murder of her husband. On the other hand, Herries and the Bishop of Ross, acting as advocates for Mary, maintained that the letters were forgeries and demanded that experts be called to prove this. To this day, the authenticity of these letters has remained unproved.

After an investigation lasting five months the Queen of England informed the opposing parties that as nothing had been discovered which called into question the honour of either the accusers or the accused, matters must remain *in status quo* until some new proof was brought forward by either of the contesting parties. As a logical sequel to this extraordinary decision Elizabeth should have sent the Regent back to Scotland and allowed Mary to be free to go where she pleased. But, instead, she was transferred from Bolton Castle to the castle in Carlisle from where, as if to crown her sorrow, the poor Queen could see the blue-shaded hills of her own Scotland.

Among the judges appointed by Elizabeth to investigate Mary's conduct was Thomas Howard, Duke of Norfolk. Whether he was honestly convinced of her innocence or was influenced by the ambitious schemes which were subsequently made the grounds of an accusation against him, and which was supposed to be none other than his own marriage to Mary, the betrothal of his daughter to the young future King, and his own appointment as Regent of Scotland, he resolved to release the Queen from imprisonment. A number of the English nobility, among them the Earls of Westmoreland and Cumberland, joined in the plot. But their plans were betrayed to the Regent who advised Elizabeth, and Norfolk's arrest was ordered. Westmoreland and Cumberland were warned in time and crossed the frontier into the Scottish Marches which were populated by Mary's supporters. The former fled from there to Flanders where he died in exile; Cumberland was betrayed to Murray and was imprisoned in Lochleven Castle where closer watch was kept over him than its previous royal prisoner. Norfolk was beheaded—Mary's star had not lost its baneful influence.

The Regent had by now returned to Edinburgh, loaded with gifts and to all intents and purposes victor in his suit since Mary remained a prisoner. He immediately set about the dispersal of her remaining partisans and, as soon as the gates of Lochleven Castle had closed upon Cumberland, he instituted proceedings in the name of the young Prince James against all those who had supported his mother's cause, and in particular the Hamiltons who, since the affair of the "street sweeping" at Edinburgh, had been mortal enemies of the Douglases. Six of the most prominent members of the family were condemned to death, but succeeded in having their sentence commuted to perpetual banishment through the intercession of John Knox, whose influence in Scotland was then so great that Murray dared not refuse him.

One of these amnestied men was a certain Hamilton of Bothwellhaugh, a true Scot of earlier days, wild and vindictive like the nobles of the time of James I. He was living in hiding in the Highlands when he learned that Murray, who had given his property to one of his favourites by virtue of confiscation against the exiles, had most cruelly thrown his sick and bedridden wife out of her own house without so much as giving her time to dress, even although it was the coldest time of the year. The poor woman, deprived of shelter, clothing or food, had gone mad and wandered about in the neighbourhood for some time. She became an object of universal pity, but of terror as well, for no-one was willing to compromise himself by doing anything to help her. She finally died of starvation and exposure at the door of the very house from which she had been driven.

When Bothwellhaugh learned of this, despite his violent nature, he showed no sign of anger other than quietly saying with a sardonic smile, "I will avenge her."

Next day he left the Highlands armed with an order from the Archbishop of St Andrews, who had followed closely the Queen's fortunes, that a house which he owned at Linlithgow should be placed at Bothwellhaugh's disposal. This house, in the main street, had a wooden balcony overlooking the square and a gate at the rear opening on to fields. Bothwellhaugh entered the house during the night, took up his quarters on the first floor, spread a black cloth over the walls so that his shadow could not be seen from outside, covered the floor with mattresses so that his steps could not be heard from the street, tied a fast horse saddled and bridled in the garden, hollowed out the arch of the little gate leading into the fields so that he could dash through at a gallop, loaded an arquebus, and shut himself up in his room.

All these preparations were due to the fact that Murray was to pass through Linlithgow on the following day. Secretly though Bothwellhaugh had worked his preparations they very nearly came to nothing, for the Regent's friends had warned him that it would be unsafe for him to pass through the village which belonged almost entirely to the Hamiltons, and advised him to make a detour to avoid it. But Murray was a brave man and not in the habit of retreating from real or suspected danger. He scoffed at what he regarded as something fanciful and refused to alter his route.

He rode down the street over which the Archbishop's balcony hung, not at a gallop and preceded by soldiers to clear the way for him, but at the snail's pace made necessary by the large crowd thronging the street to catch a glimpse of him. When he arrived opposite the balcony, as if chance favoured the murderer, the press became so great that he was forced to stop for a moment. Consequently Bothwellhaugh was able to take sure aim. He rested his arquebus on the balcony rail and, with the utmost deliberacy and coolness, fired. The gun was so heavily charged that the ball after passing through the Regent's chest killed the horse of a rider on his right. Murray fell instantly, crying: "My God! I am killed."

As the window from which the shot was fired could be clearly seen, the Regent's men at once rushed at the street door of the house and broke it down. But they were just in time to see Bothwellhaugh riding out through the garden-gate on the horse which stood ready for him. They remounted their own horses which they had left in the street and raced across the fields in pursuit. Bothwellhaugh's excellent horse had a good lead on the pursuers, but four of them, with pistolets in hand and even better mounted, began to gain ground. Seeing that whip and spurs were not enough Bothwellhaugh used his dagger to urge the horse on. Under this stimulus the animal gained fresh strength and leaped across an eighteen feet wide gully, putting a barrier between his master and the pursuers which they did not dare to attempt to leap.

The murderer found refuge in France where he was protected by the Guises. His exploit had gained him such a reputation that shortly before Saint Bartholomew's Eve overtures were made to him to assassinate Coligny. But Bothwellhaugh indignantly rejected them, saying that he avenged wrongs done to himself and was no assassin. Those who had grievances against the Admiral had only to come and ask him what were his methods and then go and do likewise.

Murray died during the night after he was wounded,

leaving the Regency to the Earl of Lennox, Darnley's father. When she learned that Murray was dead, Elizabeth cried out that she had lost her best friend.

While these events were taking place in Scotland, Mary remained a prisoner despite the incessant and urgent demands from Charles IX and Henri III. But Elizabeth, alarmed at the attempt which had been made on Mary's behalf, ordered her removal to Sheffield Castle around which guards, frequently changed, constantly patrolled.

The days, the months, and the years rolled by and poor Mary who had found it so hard to bear eleven months imprisonment at Lochleven was for fifteen or sixteen years dragged from prison to prison despite her own remonstrances and those of the French and Spanish ambassadors. She was finally consigned to Tutbury Castle under the custody of Sir Amyas Paulett, the last of her many gaolers. The quarters assigned to her there comprised two low, damp rooms where the little strength which remained to her gradually ebbed away. There were days when she could not walk because of the pain in her legs. Finally, she who had been queen of two kingdoms, rocked in a gilded cradle, and raised among velvet and silks, was compelled to humble herself so far as to beg her gaoler for a softer bed and warmer bed coverings. This simple request was treated as if it were a matter of state importance and gave rise to negotiations which lasted a month before her request was granted.

Despite the unhealthiness of her place of confinement, the cold, the privations of every kind, her robust constitution still resisted. Paulett was made to understand how great a service he would be rendering his Queen by shortening the life of the rival who was already condemned to death in her mind but was so slow to die. But Sir Amyas, coarse and hard as he was in his treatment of Mary, swore that so long as she was in his charge she need have no fear of poison or dagger, for he would himself taste all the food which was served to her and no person would come near her except when he was present. In fact, some assassins sent by Leicester, who had aspired briefly to marry the lovely Mary Stuart, were driven from the castle by its angry governor as soon as he learned the object of their visit.

So Elizabeth was obliged to possess her soul in patience, and to content herself with tormenting her whom she could not murder, with the hope that some new opportunity would present itself to bring her to trial. This opportunity was long in coming, but Mary's unlucky star brought it about at last.

A young Roman Catholic gentleman of fortune, the last remnant of the old-fashioned chivalry almost extinct by that time, was raised to such a pitch of fervour by the Pope's excommunication which declared that Elizabeth had forfeited her throne and hopes of heavenly salvation, that he resolved to restore Mary to liberty. By then she was beginning to be regarded rather as a martyr to her faith than as a political prisoner.

A law had been enacted by Elizabeth in 1585 which provided that if any attack should be contemplated or made on her person by or on behalf of anybody *who assumed to have a claim on the English throne*, a commission comprising twenty-five members should be appointed which would have exclusive jurisdiction to investigate the offence and to sentence the culprits, whomsoever they might be.

This man Babington, not discouraged by the example of his predecessors, collected five of his friends who were zealous Catholics like himself. They put their lives and honour at stake in the plot in which he was the prime mover to assassinate Elizabeth and raise Mary Stuart to the English throne. Well-planned as the plot was, it was revealed to Walsingham who allowed the conspirators to go as far as he thought they could without danger and had them all arrested the day before that fixed for the assassination.

When this imprudent and desperate undertaking at last put her rival's fate in her hands according to the letter of the law, Elizabeth was overjoyed. Orders were at once given to Sir Amyas Paulett to seize the prisoner's papers and to transfer her to Fotheringay Castle. Paulett, with a hypocritical pretence of relaxing his usual strictness, under the pretext that her health required it, offered the Queen the opportunity of a ride on horseback. The poor prisoner, who for three years had not seen green fields except through iron bars, accepted the offer with delight and rode out of Tutbury between two guards. She was mounted for greater security on a horse that was hobbled. These two guards escorted her to Fotheringay where she found the rooms which she was to occupy draped in black. Living, she had entered her tomb. Babington and his accomplices had already been executed.

Meanwhile, Mary's two secretaries, Curle and Nane, were arrested. Elizabeth commanded the commissioners to assemble and to proceed without delay with the Queen's trial. They reached Fotheringay on the 14 October 1586, and on the following morning they assembled in the castle's great hall and began their investigation.

At first Mary refused to appear before them on the grounds that they were incompetent to judge her as they were not her peers, and challenged English law which had never afforded her the least protection but had invariably left her at the mercy of those who were more powerful than she. But when, finally, she saw that the trial proceeded in her absence and learned that calumnies of all kinds were admitted as evidence, no one being there to refute them, she reconsidered her decision.

There should be quoted now the report of the interrogations to which Mary was subjected, as sent by M. de Bellièvre to M. de Villeroy; M. de Bellièvre was an Envoy Extraordinary from Henri III to Elizabeth.

"The Queen of Scotland, having taken her seat at the end of the hall and the commissioners being seated around her, began as follows:

'I do not consider that any of you assembled here is my

equal, competent to be my judge, or to question me with reference to any charge. Therefore, all that I do and say at this moment is of my own free will, and I call on God to witness that I am innocent of the assertions and calumnies made against me and that my conscience is pure. I am a free princess and born a Queen, responsible to no one except God and to Him alone can I be called upon to render account of my actions. Therefore I renew my protest so that my appearance before you may in no way prejudice me, nor the kings, princes and potentates my allies, nor my son, and I demand that my protest be recorded and a copy be given to me.'

"Then the Chancellor, who was one of the commissioners, replied, and protested against the Queen's protest; he ordered that the commission under which they were proceeding be read to the Queen, and which, he claimed, was founded upon the statutes and laws of the Kingdom.

"To this Mary replied with a further protest to the effect that these statutes and laws were without force against her because they were never intended to apply to persons of her rank.

"The Chancellor's reply to this was that the commission was ordered to proceed against her, even though she refused to plead, and declared that they would have done so in view of the fact that she came within both provisions of the law— the conspiracy having not only been formed in her interest, but also with her consent. To which the Queen replied that such a thought had never entered her mind. At this point letters purporting to have been written by her to Babington, and his replies, were read to her.

"Mary Stuart then declared that she had never seen Babington and never conferred with him, that never in her life had she ever received a letter from him and that she defied anyone in the world to prove that she had ever done anything prejudicial or hostile to the Queen of England. Furthermore, she reminded her judges that being so closely guarded, beyond reach of all news, separated and cut off from her kindred, surrounded by enemies, and deprived of anyone who could advise her, she could neither have participated in nor consented to the intrigues of which she was accused. She said that many persons whom she did not know wrote to her and that she received many letters that came from she knew not where.

"Babington's confession was then read to her, but she replied that she did not know what he meant—if Babington and his accomplices had really said such things then they were cowards, forgers and liars.

'Since you say I have written to Babington', she exclaimed, 'show me my handwriting and my signature, and not false copies like these which you have filled at your leisure with whatever falsehoods it pleased you to put in them.'

"She was then shown the letter which they said Babington had written to her. She glanced over it and said:

'I know nothing of this letter.'

"They then showed her her alleged reply, and she again said,

'Nor do I know anything of this. If you can show me a letter in my own writing, with my signature, containing what you claim, I will agree to everything; but, as I have already said, up to the present you have produced no credible evidence, nothing but these forgeries of your own invention, concocted to please yourselves.'

"With that she rose and with eyes full of tears she said,

'If I have ever consented to this or other similar intrigues, having in view the death of my sister queen, I pray that God will have neither compassion nor mercy for me. I confess having written to several people begging them to take counsel how they might deliver me from my wretched captivity, for I have languished in prison, a captive, ill-used princess, for nineteen years and seven months. But it has never occurred to me to write or wish such things against the Queen. Yes, I confess that I have done what I was able to do to secure the release of some persecuted Catholics and if I had been able then, or were able now, to save them by shedding my own blood, I should have and would still do so.'

"Then, turning towards Walsingham, she continued, 'From the moment I saw you here, my lord, I knew from whence this blow came. You have always been my most bitter enemy, and my son's, and you have prejudiced everyone against me.'

"Thus directly accused Walsingham rose.

'Madam,' he replied, 'I declare before God, who is my witness, that you are mistaken and that I have done nothing against you unworthy of a man of honour or as a public servant.'

"That was all that was said and done on this first day. On the following day the Queen was again brought before the commissioners, and having once again taken her seat at the table with the commissioners around her as before, she began by saying in a clear voice:

'You are well aware, my lords and gentlemen, that I am a sovereign Queen, anointed and consecrated in the house of God, and that I neither can nor should, for any cause whatsoever, be summoned to your presence nor be made to stand at your bar, to be judged by the laws and statutes which you quote. For I am a free-born princess and owe to no prince more than he owes me, and as for all of this of which I am accused against my sister I cannot reply properly unless you give me permission to have the assistance of my counsel. If you proceed, do as you will. But for all your judgments, in repeating my protestations I appeal to God, the only just and true judge, and to the kings and princes who are my peers.'

"This protest was also recorded in accordance with her demands.

"She was then accused of having written a number of letters to the princes of Christendom railing against England and England's Queen.

'As for that,' Mary replied, 'it is another matter, and I do not deny it. If it were to be done again I would do it, as I did before, in furtherance of my search for liberty. Nor is there any man or woman in the world, of whatever rank, who would not do as much and would not resort to the assistance of their friends to obtain release from a captivity as cruel as mine. You accuse me on the evidence of certain letters of Babington's; I do not deny now that he wrote to me and that I replied, but if you can find in my replies one single word about the Queen, my sister, then I admit the justice of these proceedings against me. I wrote that I would accept his offer to set me free if he could do it without compromising either of us. That is all. As for my secretaries it was not them but the torture which spoke. Nor is there great reliance to be placed on the confessions of Babington and his accomplices, for now that they are dead you can put what words you like into their mouths, and those who choose to do so can believe you.'

"Having said this the Queen refused to answer further questions unless she was allowed counsel, and after renewing her protest withdrew to her rooms. But, as Walsingham had threatened, the trial went on in her absence."

Meanwhile, Monsieur de Chateauneuf, the French Ambassador in London, was too close to the palace to be deceived as to the course affairs were taking. Consequently, when the first news reached him that Mary was to be brought to trial, he wrote to Henri III urging him to intervene on behalf of the prisoner. Henri at once sent M. de Bellièvre as Envoy Extraordinary to Elizabeth.

At the same time, having been informed that Mary's son, instead of interesting himself in his mother's fate, had replied to Courcelles, the French Ambassador to Scotland, when he ventured to speak to him of her, "I can do nothing; let her drink what she poured out for herself." Henri wrote the following letter to Courcelles in the hope of making James decide to help him in the efforts that he proposed making.

Courcelles: We have received your letter of the 4th
October and have read the observations of the King of
Scotland in response to the assurance you gave him of
our affection for him, observations which tend to show
that he is disposed to reciprocate that feeling; but we
would wish that your letter had informed us that he was
more kindly disposed towards the Queen, his mother,
and that his heart prompted him to arrange matters in
such a way as to assist her in her present affliction, for the
fact that she has been unjustly imprisoned for over
eighteen years ought to induce him to lend a willing ear
to any plans which have been proposed to him to secure
her freedom. Liberty is naturally desired by all men, and
above all by those who are born sovereign and destined
to rule over other men. He ought also to consider that
if our good sister, the Queen of England, hearkens to the
counsels of those who desire that she should stain her
hands with Queen Mary's blood it will lastingly dis-
honour him as the universal judgment of mankind will
be that he refused to give his mother the benefit of his
good offices with the Queen of England as he should
have done, and which would, perhaps, suffice to move
her if he had chosen to make them with the earnestness
which his filial duty would seem to demand. Furthermore, it is to be feared that, his mother dead, his turn
will come, and that they might think to rid themselves
of him by violence in order to make it a simpler matter
for those who assert their claims to the English accession
after Elizabeth's death, not only to frustrate the King of
Scotland of his rightful claim to the throne of England,
but to cast suspicions on his right to his own crown.
We do not know in what state our sister-in-law may be
when you receive this letter; but we will say this, that in
any event we wish you to do your utmost by urgent
remonstrance, and in every other way which occurs to

you, to arouse the King of Scotland to exert himself to defend and protect his mother. That you should say to him from us that as it is something for which, should he do it, he will be commended enthusiastically by all other kings and sovereign princes, so must he be assured that if he fail in this duty he will be severely blamed and the result may be disastrous to his own interests. Further, as to our own affairs, you will learn from this that the Queen, our mother, is soon to meet the King of Navarre and to confer with him with a view to composing the disorders of the realm; if his affection for us is as great as ours for him we hope that matters will soon be brought to a satisfactory conclusion, and that our subjects will have some respite from the grievous ills and calamities resulting from a civil war. We pray that the Creator, Courcelles, will have you in His Holy keeping.

Done at Saint-Germain-en-Laye, the 21st November 1586

Signed, Henri
Countersigned, Brulart

This letter at last aroused James to make a feeble effort on his mother's behalf. He sent Gray, Robert Melville, and Keith to Queen Elizabeth. But although Edinburgh was much nearer London than Paris the French envoys arrived there before the Scots.

It is true that when M. de Bellièvre reached Calais on the twenty-seventh of November, he found there a messenger from M. de Chateauneuf urging him not to lose a moment. In order to facilitate his journey the Ambassador had chartered a vessel which was lying in the harbour ready to sail. However, despite their anxiety to make all speed, they had to wait on the wind which did not allow them to put to sea until midnight on Friday, the twenty-eighth. When they reached Dover at nine the following morning they were so prostrated by seasickness that they had to stay the whole day in that town to recover. It was not until Sunday, the thirtieth, therefore, that M. de Bellièvre set out for London in the vehicle provided for him by M. de Chateauneuf through M. de Brancaléon and accompanied by the gentlemen of his suite mounted on post-horses. But they made up for the lost time by their few halts on the road and finally reached London at mid-day on Monday the first of December. M. de Bellièvre immediately sent one of his suite, M. de Villiers, to the Queen who was then in court at Richmond. The judgment had already been secretly pronounced six days previously, and had been submitted to Parliament which was debating it behind closed doors.

The French envoy could not have asked for an audience of Elizabeth at a more unfortunate moment. To gain time she refused to receive de Villiers, sending word that the reason for her refusal would be given to him next day. When the next day came the rumour was generally current in London that the French envoy had contracted the plague and that two members of his suite had died from it in Calais. For that reason, in spite of her desire to oblige Henri III, the Queen could not expose her valuable life to the risk of contagion by receiving his envoy.

M. de Bellièvre's astonishment when he heard of this was unbounded. He protested that the Queen had been misled by a false report and insisted on being received. Nevertheless the audience was postponed for six days, and as he threatened to wait no longer, Elizabeth, disturbed by Spain's attitude and not anxious to embroil herself with France, sent word to him on the morning of the seventh of December that she would receive him with his suite at Richmond that evening.

At the appointed hour the French delegation presented itself at the palace gates and were conducted into the Queen's presence. They found her seated and surrounded by the most eminent members of her court. Messieurs de Chateauneuf and de Bellièvre, having saluted her in the name of the King of France, began by delivering the formal protest which they had been instructed to do.

Elizabeth replied in excellent French. She spoke with passion as she pointed out to the delegation that the Queen of Scotland had always endangered her and that this was the third time she had attempted her life by various strategies, all of which she had endured with considerable patience. But nothing in all her life had ever wounded her so deeply as this latest conspiracy which, she added sadly, had cost her more sighs and tears than the loss of her parents. It was especially grievous, she said, because the Queen of Scotland was so closely related to herself as well as to the King of France. Since Messieurs de Chateauneuf and de Bellièvre had cited in their protests several examples drawn from history, she continued in her customary pedantic tone when she came to reply to that part of their harangue, saying that she had seen and read many books in her life, more indeed than the majority of women in her rank were accustomed to do, but that she had never found in all her reading one single instance of an act like that which had been planned against her, planned, moreover, by her own kinswoman whom the King, her brother, could not and should not support in her treachery, for it was his duty to hasten the punishment which was her due. Then she addressed herself particularly to M. de Bellièvre. Putting aside her arrogance and assuming a gracious air, she said that she deeply regretted that he had not come as an envoy for happier reasons and that in a few days she would hand her reply to her brother Henri, as to whose health she enquired solicitously, as well as that of the Queen Mother, who, she said, must be thoroughly exhausted by her efforts to restore peace in her son's realm. Then, not wishing to say anything further she withdrew from the room.

The deputation returned to London and there awaited the promised reply. While they were doing this they learned from a secret source that sentence of death had been passed on Mary. This information determined them to return to Richmond and remonstrate further with the Queen. After making two or three profitless journeys they were at last admitted for the second time to the Queen's presence on the fifteenth of December. Elizabeth did not deny that sentence of death had been pronounced, and it was very easy to see that she did not intend to exercise her prerogative of pardon. M. de Bellièvre concluded that his mission was hopeless and asked for his "safe-conduct" to be returned to him. Elizabeth promised to let him have these papers in two or three days.

On the following Tuesday, the seventeenth of December, Parliament was convoked at the Palace of Westminster and there, to a full house, the proclamation was made announcing that Mary Stuart had been condemned to death. Immediately, that sentence of death was read with much pomp and solemnity in all the squares and public places in London. The news spread throughout England. Bells were rung for twenty-four hours and strict orders were issued to all citizens to light bonfires in their streets.

Amid the clamour of the bells and in the glare of the fires M. de Bellièvre determined to make one last effort so that he should have nothing with which to reproach himself and wrote the following letter to Queen Elizabeth:

Madam, we left Your Majesty's presence yesterday when you were graciously pleased to promise us that we should within a few days receive your reply to our royal master's prayer on behalf of the Queen of Scotland, his sister-in-law and ally. But we have this morning been advised that the said Queen's sentence has been publicly proclaimed throughout London, although we based other hopes upon your clemency and the friendship you bear for our King. Nevertheless, to neglect nothing which we believe is our duty and to fulfil the intentions of our King, our master, we do hereby again humbly implore Your Majesty not to refuse His Majesty's most urgent and most affectionate prayer that it may please you to spare the life of the Queen of Scotland, which our master the King will receive as the greatest favour Your Majesty could bestow upon him. Just as, on the other hand, nothing could happen which could cause him greater displeasure, or wound him more deeply, than the proposed treatment of the said Queen, she being as she is made. And, Madam, as our King, our master and your good brother, when he accredited us to Your Majesty on his behalf did not consider it possible that such a dénoument could be reached so speedily, we must humbly implore you, Madam, before the irrevocable step is taken to allow us sufficient time in which to inform him of the plight of the Queen of Scotland so that, before Your Majesty comes to a final determination on the matter, you may know what His Most Christian Majesty may be pleased to say to you by way of remonstrance concerning the most important affair which, within our memory, has been submitted to the judgment of men. Monsieur de Saint-Cyr who will present this to Your Majesty will bring us, we venture to hope, a favourable reply.

London, the 16th day of December 1586

Signed, de Bellièvre

(and) de l'Aubespine Chateauneuf

On the same day, M. de Saint-Cyr, accompanied by other members of the Embassy, took this letter to Richmond. But the Queen declined to receive them, giving the excuse that she was indisposed. They were compelled to hand their letter to Walsingham, who promised to send the Queen's reply the following day.

In spite of this promise the French delegation were made to wait for two days. At last, towards the evening of the second day, two Englishmen called upon M. de Bellièvre. Without showing him anything in writing to confirm what they said, they told him on the Queen's behalf that in reply to the letter, and to indulge the wish they expressed for a reprieve so that they might communicate this to the King of France, Her Majesty had decided to agree to a reprieve of twelve days. As this was Elizabeth's final word, and it was useless to waste time in pressing the matter further, M. de Genlis was at once dispatched to Henri III with instructions to supplement the long dispatch of de Chateauneuf and de Bellièvre by telling him orally all that he had seen and heard relative to Queen Mary's affairs during his stay in England.

Henri III at once replied with a letter containing fresh instructions for de Chateauneuf and de Bellièvre, but although M. de Genlis made the utmost haste he did not reach London until the fourteenth day, forty-eight hours after the expiration of the reprieve. Nevertheless, as the sentence had not been carried out, de Chateauneuf and de Bellièvre at once set out for Greenwich, where the court was in residence for the Christmas season to request an audience when they could give to Elizabeth their King's reply. For several days they were unsuccessful, but as they refused to be rebuffed and returned again and again, they were finally granted an audience on the sixth of January.

As on previous occasions they were ushered in with all the strict formalities of court etiquette and found Elizabeth awaiting them in the audience hall. The two men approached and bowed and, de Bellièvre addressing her respectfully but firmly, began to remonstrate with her in the King's name. Elizabeth listened impatiently moving restlessly in her chair, and at last, unable to control herself, she rose, her cheeks flaming, and burst out,

"Monsieur de Bellièvre, have you been charged by your King, my brother, to use such language to us?"

"Yes, Your Majesty," he replied, bowing, "I have his express commands to do so."

"Have you them in writing and signed by him?"

"Yes, Madam," The envoy replied, still with perfect coolness, "the King, your brother, expressly instructed me in letters signed with his own hand to address to Your Majesty the remonstrances I have had the honour to make to you."

"In that case," cried Elizabeth, giving free rein to her anger, "we demand copies of such letters attested with your own signature, and rest assured that you will answer for every word which you expunge or add."

"Madam, it is not the practice of Kings of France or their agents to falsify either letters or documents, and tomorrow morning you shall have the copies you demand. I will answer for their accuracy."

"Enough, Monsieur, enough," the Queen exclaimed, and signing to members of her court to leave the hall, she remained for nearly an hour closeted with the Ambassador and the envoy.

No one knows what passed at that interview except that the Queen undertook to send an envoy to Henri III and promised that he would reach Paris as soon as de Bellièvre, if not in advance of him, and would be the bearer of her final decision regarding the Queen of Scotland. Elizabeth then withdrew, giving the two men fully to understand that any further attempts that they might make to see her would be fruitless.

On the thirteenth of January, the French mission received their "safe conducts" and at the same time were told that a naval ship was awaiting them at Dover.

On the very day of their departure a strange thing happened. A man by the name of Stafford, brother of Elizabeth's Ambassador to France, called on M. de Trappes, an attaché of the French Embassy in London, and said that he knew of a man imprisoned for debt who had something of the highest importance to communicate to him. To arouse his interest even more, he added that this something was connected with the good offices of the King of France relating to the affairs of the Queen of Scotland. Although M. de Trappes at first regarded this information with suspicion, he felt that in the existing circumstances he had no right to be influenced by mere suspicion and thus to have any reason for reproaching himself in a matter of such urgency. He therefore went with Stafford to the prison where the man was detained.

When they met, the prisoner told M. de Trappes that he was imprisoned for a debt of only twenty crowns. His longing for freedom was so great that if M. de Chateauneuf would pay the debt for him he would undertake to rescue the Queen of Scotland from her present peril by stabbing Queen Elizabeth. At this suggestion M. de Trappes, seeing the trap that was set for his Ambassador, expressed his unbounded astonishment and said that he was positive that M. de Chateauneuf would be horrified at the idea of any plot which included an attempt on the Queen of England's life, or the slightest disturbance of the tranquillity of her kingdom. Then, refusing to listen further, he hurried back to report to M. de Chateauneuf all that had taken place.

The Ambassador immediately understood the motive behind the proposal and said to Stafford that it seemed extraordinary that a man such as he should dare to suggest to him such frightful treason, and ordered him to leave the Embassy at once and never to return. Stafford left the room and, pretending to believe that he was a lost man, begged M. de Trappes to allow him to join the French envoys and cross the Channel. This request was referred to the Ambassador whose reply was that not only was Stafford forbidden ever to enter the Embassy again but also that he must have no communication of any sort with any member of the staff; it was thus made plain that his request could not be considered. For good measure M. de Chateauneuf added that if he were not restrained by his high regard for his fellow diplomat, the Earl of Stafford, he would denounce him at once to Elizabeth.

On that same day Stafford was arrested.

After this incident M. de Trappes set out to overtake his compatriots who had left several hours previously. Just as he arrived at Dover he was arrested, taken back to London, and imprisoned. Interrogated the same day he related frankly everything that had happened, appealing to M. de Chateauneuf to confirm what he had said. He was interrogated again on the following day and his amazement was great when, in answer to his request that his replies of the previous day should be read back to him, there were produced only falsified copies which compromised both the Ambassador and himself. Indignantly, he entered a formal protest, refused to answer further questions, and was taken back to the Tower with redoubled precautions intended to give the impression that he was being held on a most serious charge.

The next day the Ambassador was summoned before the Queen and was confronted with Stafford who had the impudence to insist that M. de Chateauneuf was concerned in a plot with M. de Trappes and a man imprisoned for debt, and that the plot was aimed at nothing less than the Queen's life. The Ambassador denied all this heatedly and indignantly—but Elizabeth was too deeply interested in not being convinced to allow the strongest evidence to convince her. She told M. de Chateauneuf that only his diplomatic immunity saved him from being arrested like his confederate M. de Trappes. She sent immediately, as she had promised to do, an envoy to Henri III, but he was instructed not to explain to him the judgment pronounced on Mary and the execution which was soon to follow, but only to accuse M. de Chateauneuf with complicity in a plot the discovery of which had determined the Queen of Scotland's fate. She was finally convinced that her own existence would be threatened every hour so long as her enemy remained alive.

That very day Elizabeth took measures to spread, not only in London but throughout England, the report of the latest danger from which she had escaped. Thus, when the Scottish envoys ultimately arrived in London two days after the departure of the French mission, the Queen told them that their request for clemency was particularly ill-timed—for she had just gained convincing proof that her life was in jeopardy as long as Mary Stuart lived. Robert Melville tried to reply, upon which Elizabeth lost her temper and said that it was he who gave James the bad advice to interest himself on his mother's behalf, and that if she had had such an adviser she would have him beheaded.

To this Melville replied that he would never, even at the risk of his own life, refrain from offering his master good advice and that, on the contrary, it would be more just to say that the man who would advise a son to abandon his mother and leave her to die without a protest deserved the beheading. At that Elizabeth ordered them to withdraw, saying that she would communicate her reply to them.

Several days having passed with no message being brought, they requested an audience to learn the Queen's final decision. An audience was granted and, as in the case of M. de Bellièvre, it consisted of recriminations and complaints. Finally Elizabeth demanded of them what assurance they would give her of her own safety if she should consent to pardon the Queen of Scotland. The envoys replied that they were authorized in the name of their master and all the nobility of his kingdom that Mary Stuart would renounce the crown in favour of her son, all her rights to the English throne, and that the King of France and all her relatives and friends among the princes and nobles would be her sureties.

To this, forgetting her usual presence of mind, she exclaimed, "What do you say, Melville? That would be to arm our enemy with two claims whereas he has now only one!"

"Then does Your Majesty regard my master as your enemy?" Melville replied. "He believed that he was more fortunate, Madam, and that he was your ally."

"No, no," said Elizabeth, colouring, "that was a mere figure of speech, and if you can find a way of conciliating everyone, gentlemen, we are ready to err on the side of clemency to prove to you that we regard your master as our good and faithful ally. Do you think out a way of settlement and we, for our part, will do our best to find one."

With this she left the room, and the envoys withdrew with a faint spark of hope kindled in them.

That evening a member of Elizabeth's court called upon Mr Gray, secretary to the Scottish Ambassador, apparently on no other than a social visit. In the course of conversation he said that it was very difficult to reconcile Queen Elizabeth's safety with the life of her prisoner, and furthermore that if the Queen of Scotland should be pardoned and either she or her son ever sat on the English throne there would be no security for those members of the commission who had voted for her death. There was only one way of adjusting the matter, and that was for James to renounce his own claim to the crown of England, otherwise Queen Elizabeth could never dare spare Queen Mary's life with a proper regard to her own safety.

Looking at his visitor squarely in the face Gray asked him if his sovereign had instructed him to speak as he had done. The reply was a disclaimer of any authority on the matter and that they were entirely personal views advanced only as advice.

At the final audience given to the Scottish envoys Elizabeth said to them that, after much reflection, she had discovered no way of assuring her own safety and sparing the Queen of Scotland's life, and consequently she was unable to grant their master's request. After this pronouncement Melville replied that if that were a final decision his orders required him to formally protest that the entire proceeding against Mary Stuart was null and void because the Queen of England had no jurisdiction over one who was a queen like herself and her equal in birth and rank. Consequently, immediately on their return to Scotland and when their master had learned of the failure of their mission, he would convoke his Parliament and send messengers to all the princes in Christendom to concert measures with them to avenge her whom they had failed to save.

Elizabeth at once flew into a new rage. She said that they were certainly not commissioned by their master to speak in such manner to her. But they offered to confirm their declaration in writing, and signed by them. To this Elizabeth replied that she would send an envoy who would arrange everything with her good friend and ally the future King of Scotland. Melville then told her that his master would listen to no one until his envoys had returned, at which she requested them not to leave hastily as she had not as yet arrived at any irrevocable decision.

During the evening following this audience Lord Highley called on Gray and commented admiringly upon a handsome pair of Italian pistolets. A little later Gray handed them to a cousin of Highley and asked him to take them to him with his compliments. The young man was very pleased to do so and went at once to the royal palace, where his kinsman had rooms, to deliver the gift which had been entrusted to him. He had scarcely entered the palace when he was stopped and searched, and the weapons being found upon him, although they were not loaded, he was at once arrested. Instead of taking him to the Tower he was locked up in a room.

The next day it was currently reported that the Scottish envoys had, in their turn, taken to planning the assassination of the Queen and that weapons provided by Gray himself had been found on a would-be murderer. Bad faith was so obvious in this affair that the Scots were convinced that they could do nothing for poor Mary Stuart and, reluctantly abandoning her to her fate, they left for Scotland on the following day.

Directly they were gone Elizabeth sent Davison, a secretary, to Sir Amyas Paulett. He was instructed to sound him afresh with regard to his prisoner. In spite of herself the Queen was fearful at the thought of a public execution and reverted to her original thinking of poisoning or assassination. But Sir Amyas said forcibly that no person except the executioner would be admitted to Mary's presence, and that even he must be provided with a proper warrant. Davison reported back to Elizabeth, who stamped her foot impatiently as she listened, and when he had finished, could not restrain her anger.

"God's death!" she cried out, "what a scrupulous rascal he is. He talks incessantly of his fidelity yet refuses to prove it."

Elizabeth was forced at last to come to some decision. She demanded a death warrant from Davison, and when he gave it to her she signed it without a tremor, forgetting that she was herself the daughter of a queen who had died on the scaffold. Having ordered the Great Seal of England to be affixed she said laughingly, "Now go and tell Walsingham that all is over for poor Queen Mary. But break the news to him gently for he is ill, and I fear the shock may kill him."

Her pleasantry was the more atrocious as it was well-known that Walsingham was the Queen of Scotland's most implacable enemy.

Towards the evening of the same day, a Saturday, a man named Beale, who was Walsingham's brother-in-law, was summoned to the palace. The Queen handed him the death warrant and with it an order addressed to the Earls of Shrewsbury, Kent and Rutland, and other noblemen whose estates were in the neighbourhood of Fotheringay, to be present at the execution. Beale took the executioner with him from London, and in accordance with the Queen's command he was to be dressed in black velvet for the great occasion. They set out two hours after receiving their instructions.

For the past two months Queen Mary had been aware of the finding of the commissioners. On the day that judgment was passed she was told of it by her confessor who was allowed to see her only on that occasion. She took advantage of his visit to hand to him three letters which she wrote in his presence—one to Pope Sixtus V, one to Don Bernado Mendoza, and the third, which ran as follows, to the duc de Guise:

4th December 1586

My dearest cousin, this is to bid you farewell for I am on the point of being put to death by virtue of an unjust judgment, and to such a death as no one of our family, thank God, and never a queen or one of lower rank has ever suffered. But, my good cousin, give praise to the Lord for I am of no use in this world to the cause of God and His church, prisoner as I am; on the other hand I hope that my death will bear witness to the constancy of my faith and my willingness to suffer for the maintenance and restoration of the Catholic church in this unfortunate island. And although no executioner has ever before laid hands on one of our blood, be not ashamed of my death, for the judgment of heretics who have no jurisdiction over me, a Queen in her own right, will be of profit in God's sight to the children of His church. If I should have consented, however, to what they proposed to me, I would not have been brought to this pass. Our whole family has been persecuted by these fanatics, for example your good father, through whose intercession I hope to receive forgiveness from the Almighty Judge. I commend my poor attendants to your care, and ask you to pay my debts, and to provide for a regular anniversary mass for the repose of my soul, not at your expense but by contributions and royal ordinance as you will feel called upon to do when you have learned my wishes from the poor and devoted servants who will be witness to my final tragedy. May God prosper you, your wife, children, brothers and cousins, and especially the head of our house, my good brother and cousin. May God's blessing be on your children whom I commend to His blessing no less earnestly than my own son, unfortunate and deluded as he may be. You will receive certain of my rings which will remind you to pray to God for the soul of your poor cousin who is without assistance or counsel other than that of our Lord who gives her strength and courage to stand alone against the wolves who howl for her blood. To God be the glory.

Pray pay particular heed to what will be told you by the person who will give you my ruby ring, for I take it on my conscience that he will faithfully tell you the truth on the matter with which I have charged him, and especially that portion which relates to my poor attendants and the interests of one of them. I commend that person to you for her perfect sincerity and honesty, hoping that some fitting position may be provided for her. I have chosen her for her impartiality and the one who will convey my wishes to you accurately. Do not let anyone know, I beg, that she has a special mission for the envy of others would be her ruin. These last two years and more I have suffered much, but have not been able to let you know for a very important reason. God be praised for all His works and give you grace to persevere in the service of His church as long as you live, and may our family never lose the honour of always being ready, women as well as men, to shed our blood in fighting the battles of the faith, leaving all worldly considerations aside. As for myself, I consider that my birth both on my father's and on my mother's side, makes it incumbent on me to offer my blood in that behalf, and I do not intend to fail in my duty. May Jesus who was crucified for us, and all the martyred saints, intercede to make us worthy to offer our earthly bodies as voluntary sacrifices to His glory.

From Fotheringay, Thursday the 24th of November. Thinking to humble me, they cut down the canopy over my altar, and my keeper afterwards came and offered to write to the Queen saying that it was not done on his orders but on the advice of some of the council. I had shown the Cross of our Blessed Lord upon the canopy instead of our royal arms. You will hear the whole story; since then my treatment has been gentle.

Your loving cousin and devoted friend
Mary, Queen of Scotland and Dowager of France

From the day when she learned of her sentence, Mary had abandoned all hope, for she knew that her life depended on Elizabeth's pardon, and thought only of making preparations for her death. The cold and the dampness of the various prisons in which she had been confined had so affected her that at times her limbs were almost paralysed, and she was haunted by the fear that she would be unable to walk resolutely to the scaffold as she intended to do. So, on Saturday the fourteenth of February, she sent for Bourgoin, her physician, and telling him that she had a presentiment that the hour of her death was imminent, asked him what she could do to prevent the aches which paralysed her. He replied that it would be advisable to purge herself with fresh herbs.

"Go then," the Queen said, "and in my name ask Sir Amyas Paulett to allow you to go into the fields and gather them."

Bourgoin went down to Sir Amyas who was himself a sufferer from sciatica, and on that account more likely to appreciate the urgency of the Queen's needs. But the request, simple as it was, met with many obstacles. Sir Amyas said that he could do nothing without referring the matter to his colleague Drury, but he would send for ink and paper and Bourgoin could then make a list of the herbs he needed and they would try to procure them for him. Bourgoin replied that he was not well enough acquainted with English, and that the village apothecaries did not know enough Latin for him to risk the Queen's life by a chance error on either side. At last, after much hesitation, Paulett allowed Bourgoin to go out accompanied by the apothecary Gorjon. On the next day the Queen began the treatment.

Mary's presentiments were only too well justified. On Tuesday the seventeenth of January, at about two in the afternoon, the Earls of Kent and Shrewsbury, accompanied by Beale, sent word to the Queen that they wished to speak to her. She replied that she was ill and in bed but if, however, they had something of serious consequence to say and they would give her a little time, she would get up. They answered that the communication which they had to make was urgent and that they, therefore, begged her to receive them. Hearing this, Mary at once got up, put on a dressing-gown, and sat at a small table where she usually passed a great deal of the day.

The two earls, accompanied by Beale, Paulett and Drury, then entered the room. They were followed by her favourite maids and confidential servants, drawn by a curiosity filled with anguish. These were Renée de Really, Gilles Maubray, Jean Kennedy, Elspeth Curle, Mary Paget and Susan Kirkcaldy, with Dominique Bourgoin, her physician, Pierre Gorjon, the apothecary, Jacques Gervais, her surgeon, Annibal Stewart, the valet, Didier Sifflart, the butler, John Lauder, the pantler, and Martin Huyet, her equerry.

The Earl of Shrewsbury, standing with uncovered head, as did all the others while they were in the Queen's presence, then addressed Mary in English:

"Madam, the Queen of England, my august mistress, has sent me to you with the Earl of Kent and Robert Beale, here present, to inform you that after an impartial investigation, you have been found guilty of the transgression of which you had been accused. The result of the investigation has already been given to Your Grace by Lord Buckhurst and the execution of the sentence having been delayed to the last possible moment the Queen can no longer resist the urging of her subjects who, in their great and affectionate fear for her safety, are pressing her to have the sentence carried out. To that end we have come, Madam, bearers of a commission and we humbly beg of you to listen to its reading."

"Read on, my lord, I am listening," Mary said tranquilly.

Thereupon Robert Beale unfolded the commission which was written on parchment and sealed with a large seal of yellow wax, and read:

"Elizabeth, by the grace of God, Queen of England, France and Ireland, etc., to our trusty and well-beloved cousins, George, Earl of Shrewsbury, Grand Marshal of England, Henry Earl of Kent, Henry, Earl of Derby, George, Earl of Cumberland, Henry, Earl of Pembroke, greetings:*

"In consequence of the sentence pronounced by us and the members of our council, nobles and judges, against the former Queen of Scotland, bearing the name of Mary, daughter and heiress of James the Fifth of Scotland, and commonly called Queen of Scotland and Dowager of France, which sentence all the states of our kingdom in our last Parliament assembled, not only ratified but after mature deliberation declared to be just and reasonable; and in consequence likewise of the urgent prayer and request of our subjects entreating us to take measures for the publication thereof, and for its execution upon her person inasmuch as they judge her to have fully merited her fate, adding that her detention in this place was and would continue to be a certain and obvious peril, not to our life alone but to themselves and their posterity, and to the public welfare of the kingdom, as well as in the matter of the Gospel and in the true religion of Christ as for the peace and tranquillity of the state, and remonstrating against further delay on our part in granting a commission to carry out the said sentence; in order amply to satisfy the prayers of our Parliament, by whom we are daily informed that all our loyal subjects, as well as of the nobility than whom no advisers could be wiser and more devoted, as well as those of humbler state out of their affectionate solicitude for our life and consequent dread of the destruction of the present divine and happy state of our kingdom if we fail to carry out the said sentence, do consent to and desire its execution, although the general and constant requests, entreaties and advice urge us in a direction contrary to

* The Earls of Cumberland, Derby and Pembroke disregarded Elizabeth's commands and attended neither the reading of the sentence nor its execution.

our natural inclination, nevertheless, being well persuaded of the weight of their continual representations as tending towards the security of our person and likewise that of every person in our kingdom; we have finally consented and given order that justice be done upon the said Mary. In consideration of our entire confidence in your faithfulness and loyalty, together with your devoted affection for our person and our common country, we command and enjoin you, upon sight hereof, to repair to Fotheringay Castle where the said Queen of Scotland now is in the keeping of our friend, loyal servant and adviser, Sir Amyas Paulett, and there to take custody of the said Queen of Scotland and see to it that by your command her execution is carried out in the presence of yourselves, Sir Amyas Paulett, and of such other officials as you shall order to be present. In witness whereof, and that the said execution may be carried out in such manner and form, at such time and place, and by such persons as you five, four, three or two, shall in your discretion deem fit, all laws, statutes, ordinances to the contrary notwithstanding, we have caused the Great Seal of England to be affixed to these presents, which shall be full and sufficient warrant forever for each and all of you, and for all who shall be present or shall do anything by your command pertaining to the execution of the said sentence.

"Done and given at our Palace of Greenwich the first day of February (10th February, new style)* in the twenty-ninth year of our reign."

Mary listened to the reading with the greatest calmness and dignity. When it was finished she crossed herself, and said,

"Welcome be all that comes in the name of God. I thank thee, oh Lord, that thou deigns to put an end to all the

---

* The change from the Julian to the Gregorian Calendar came into effect in France in 1582.

ills Thou has seen me suffer for nineteen years and more."

"Madam," said the Earl of Kent, "I beg that you will bear us no malice because of your condemnation. It was essential for the tranquillity of the state and the growth of the new religion."

"So," Mary cried joyfully, "I am to have the honour of dying for the faith of my fathers, and God deigns to accord me the glory of martyrdom. Father, I thank Thee," she continued, joining her hands in pious fervour, "that Thou permit me to make such an ending of which I am so unworthy. That, my God, is truly a proof that Thou dost love me and an assurance that Thou dost receive me in the number of Thy servants. Although the sentence had been made known to me I was greatly afraid, in view of the manner in which I have been treated for nineteen years, that I might not be so near as I am to a happy ending for I thought that your Queen would not dare to lay a hand upon me who am, by God's grace, a queen like herself, like herself a king's daughter, consecrated like herself, her nearest relative too, and like herself a grand-daughter of King Henry the Seventh, and who has had the honour of being Queen of France, of which kingdom I am still Dowager. My fear was the greater," she added, placing her hand on a New Testament which lay on the little table at her side, "because I swear on this holy book that I have never sought, consented to or desired, the death of my sister the Queen of England."

"Madam," replied the Earl of Kent, taking a step towards her and pointing at the New Testament, "that book upon which you swore is false for it is the papist version, and thus your oath has no more weight than the book upon which it was sworn."

"You are wrong, my lord, what you say may be conclusive to you but it is not to me, for I know full well that this book is a true and faithful translation of the word of God made by a wise and godly man and approved by my Church."

"Madam, Your Grace's mind has been formed on the

instruction you received in your youth and you have never inquired for yourself as to what is good or bad. It is not astonishing that you should have clung to your error when none has ever shown you the truth. For that reason, and as Your Grace has only a few hours to remain in this world and thus has no time to lose, we will with your permission send for the Dean of Peterborough, a most learned theologian. His words will prepare you for your salvation which to our great grief and that of our august Queen you endanger by persisting in these papist follies, abominations and childish antics which debar Catholics from the holy word of God and from knowledge of the truth."

"You are wrong, my lord," the Queen mildly replied, "if you think I grew thoughtlessly to womanhood in the faith of my fathers and never seriously studied a matter of such vast consequence as religion. On the contrary, I grew up surrounded by learned men who instructed me thoroughly in such matters, and I have avidly read their works ever since I have been deprived of their words. During my whole life I have never doubted, and now in the hour of my death my faith will not falter. The Earl of Shrewsbury, present with us, will tell you that at the time of my coming to England I passed one whole Lenten season, which I now repent having done, listening to your most learned theologians without being in the slightest impressed by their arguments. It would, therefore, be altogether useless, my lord," she added with a smile, "to send for the Dean of Peterborough, however learned he might be. The only favour I have to ask of you, my lord, and I should be most grateful if it be granted, is that you would kindly send me my chaplain who is kept imprisoned in this castle and who would comfort me and prepare me for death. Or, if that is impossible, any other priest, it matters not whom though it be the poor priest of a poor village, for I am no harder to please than God. I do not ask that he have learning if only he have faith."

"It is with regret, Madam," the Earl of Kent replied, "that

I am compelled to refuse Your Grace's request. To grant it would be contrary to our religion and conscience, and we would lay ourselves open to grave reproach. It is for that reason that we once more suggest the venerable Dean of Peterborough, being certain that Your Grace will derive more comfort and satisfaction from him than from any bishop, priest or vicar of the Catholic church."

"Thank you, my lord, but I do not desire to see the Dean, and as I am innocent of the crime for which I have to die, martyrdom, with God's help, will take the place of confession. And now I will venture to remind you, my lord, that I have but a few hours to die. Those few hours, if they are to be made of profit to me, should be passed in prayer and meditation and not in fruitless discussion."

With that she rose and with a courteous salute to the two earls, Beale, Paulett and Drury, she indicated with a dignified gesture that she wished to be left alone and in peace. As they were about to take their leave she said,

"Apropos, my lords, at what hour am I to prepare for death?"

"At about eight o'clock tomorrow morning, Madam," stammered the Earl of Shrewsbury.

"It is well," said Mary, "but did you bring me no reply from my sister Elizabeth to a letter which I wrote to her about a month ago?"

"To what did the letter relate, Madam, if you please?" asked the Earl of Kent.

"To my funeral and burial, my lord. I asked to be buried in France, in the cathedral at Rheims, beside the late Queen, my mother."

"That cannot be, Madam. But do not disquiet yourself about such details for my august mistress, the Queen, will make suitable provision for your obsequies. Has Your Grace any further request to make?"

"I should be glad to know whether my servants will be allowed to return to their own countries with the pittance

I may be able to give them, and which will in any event be but an inadequate return for the length of time they have spent in my service and the long imprisonment they have endured because of me."

"We have no authority to answer for that, Madam," the Earl of Kent replied, "but we think that everything will be done in accordance with your wishes. Is that all Your Grace has to ask of us?"

"Yes, my lord," said the Queen, bowing a second time, "and you may now withdraw."

"One moment, my lords, in heaven's name, one moment!" called out the aged physician, leaving the ranks of the servants and throwing himself at the feet of the two earls.

"What do you want?" Shrewsbury demanded.

"To impress upon your lordships," Bourgoin replied, weeping, "how little time you have allowed the Queen for preparation for the great trial before her. Consider her birth, and the rank, my lords, that this woman you have condemned has held among the princes of the earth and reflect if it is proper to treat her like any person of low estate. And if not for the sake of this noble Queen, my lords, let it be for our sakes, her unhappy servants who, having had the honour of living with her for so long cannot part from her so suddenly and without time for preparation. Consider this also, that a woman of her rank and condition should have some time to arrange her final affairs. What will become of her and us, in God's name, if our mistress has no time before dying to put her accounts in order and arrange her papers? She has services to pay for, pious works to provide for, and she will be forced to neglect one or the other. We know that she will give all her time to our concerns, and thus, my lords, she will neglect her own spiritual welfare.

"Grant her, therefore, a few days' grace, for our mistress is too proud to ask such a favour for herself. I ask it in the name of us all, and implore you not to refuse to a few poor servants a request which your own august Queen certainly would not refuse if they could have the honour of laying their petition at her feet."

"Is it true, Madam," Beale inquired, "that you have not made your will?"

"I have not done so, sir," the Queen answered.

"In that case, my lords," Beale continued, "it would perhaps be well to grant her a few days' respite."

"Impossible, sir," Shrewsbury interjected, "the time is fixed and we have no right to change it by so much as an hour."

"Enough, Bourgoin, enough," the Queen said, "I command you to rise."

Bourgoin obeyed, and Shrewsbury turned to Paulett who was behind him.

"Sir Amyas," he said, "we leave this lady in your keeping. You will keep her safely until our return."

With these words he left the room followed by Kent, Beale, Paulett and Drury. The Queen was left alone with her retinue.

Chapter 12

Mary turned to them with a face as serene as if the news she had just been given was trivial.

"Well," she said to Jean Kennedy, "have I not always told you that I knew perfectly well that their greatest wish was to do what they have done, and that I could see through all these manoeuvres what the ending would be? I was too great an obstacle to the progress of their false religion to be allowed to live. Come," she added, "let supper be served at once so that I may put my affairs in order."

Then, seeing that instead of obeying, her servants stood weeping and lamenting she said, smiling sadly but with dry eyes,

"My children, this is not a time for weeping. On the contrary, for if you love me you should rejoice that the Lord, in allowing me to die for His cause, relieves me from the suffering I have endured for nineteen years. For my part, I am grateful to Him for according me the privilege of dying for the glory of His church. Let everyone be patient and, while the men prepare supper, we women will pray to Him."

The men at once went out and the Queen and her women fell on their knees. When they had repeated several prayers Mary rose, and sending for what money she still possessed, counted it and divided it in portions which she put in separate purses with the names of the persons for whom they were intended written on them.

Supper was soon served and she took her place at the table with her women as she was accustomed to do, the servants standing behind the chairs or coming and going. Bourgoin waited upon her as he had been in the habit of doing since her steward had been sent away. She ate neither more nor less than usual, speaking much of the Earl of Kent and the way in which he had betrayed his zeal for the new religion by his eagerness to send to her what she described as a professor of that religion instead of a priest.

"Happily," she said laughingly, "it would have needed someone who could argue more skilfully than he to induce me to change my faith."

Meanwhile, Bourgoin stood behind her chair silently weeping. He knew that this would be the last time he would wait on her, and that at this hour tomorrow she who ate and talked so serenely would be cold and lifeless.

The meal finished, the Queen called together all her retinue and before the table was cleared poured a glass of wine. She rose and drank their healths and then asked them to drink to her salvation. A glass was then handed to each and they all knelt where they stood (so says the chronicle from which these details are taken) and drank, mingling their tears with the wine and begging her forgiveness for any faults of which they might have been guilty. Mary willingly forgave them and begged them to do as much for her, to forget any impatient moods and telling them to attribute them to her captivity. She then spoke to them at length upon their duty to God and their church, exhorting them to hold fast to their Catholic faith, and beseeching them when she was no more to live at peace and in charity with one another and to forget the petty quarrels and dissensions of the past.

When she had said all she had to say the Queen turned from the table, intending to go down to her wardrobe to look over the clothing and jewellery she had to dispose of. But Bourgoin suggested that it would be better to have all her effects brought to her bedroom as this would be less fatiguing and, moreover, would prevent the English from spying. This latter reason decided the Queen. While her servants were having their supper she had, first of all, all her dresses brought to the ante-room, took the list of them from the mistress of the wardrobe and began to write on the margin the name of the person for whom each article was intended— that person at once took the article in question and put it aside. Those things of such a nature that they could not be given away she ordered to be sold and the proceeds used to pay the expenses of her servants when they returned to their homes, for she knew that their expenses would be heavy and that none of them had the means for paying them. After she had gone through the list in this way she signed it and gave it to the mistress of the wardrobe as a sign that she might go.

The Queen then went to her bedroom where all her rings, trinkets, and most valuable personal property had been taken. She looked them all over carefully, even to those of the least value, and distributed them as she had her dresses so that everyone whether present or absent received something. To those whom she considered most trustworthy she confided the jewels which were destined for the King and Queen of France, her son, the future King of Scotland, the Queen Mother, and for Messieurs de Guise and de Lorraine; not one of her royal kindred, prince or princess, did she overlook.

She furthermore expressed the wish that each of her servants should keep such articles as had been their particular care that the linen, for instance, should go to the maid who looked after it; her embroidery to the one who had had it in charge; the silver plate to her butler; and so on. When they asked her to give them their quit-claims she said, "Such would be useless; you are responsible to no one but me and so after tomorrow you will be responsible to nobody." But when they reminded her that her son might put forward a claim, she admitted the wisdom of their request and gave them what they asked.

All this finished, and no longer having any hope that her confessor would be allowed to visit her, she wrote to him:
I have been harassed all day because of my religious beliefs and been importuned to receive the ministrations

of a heretic. You will learn from Bourgoin and the others that I was unmoved by what they said and that I made a firm declaration of the faith in which I propose to die. I asked that you might be permitted to receive my confession and administer the sacrament, but my request was cruelly refused, as well as my further request that my body should be taken to France, and that I be allowed to make my will without hindrance, so I can write nothing save under their eyes and subject to their mistress's good pleasure. Being thus prevented from seeing you I here confess my sins to you in general and not specifically as I would otherwise have done, and I beseech you in God's name to pray and watch with me this night to help me atone my sins, and to give me your absolution and forgiveness for whatever wrongs I have done. I will try to see you in their presence, as I am permitted to see my old steward and if I am successful I will ask your blessing on my knees before them all. Send me the most comforting prayers that you know for the night and tomorrow morning, for my time is short and I have not the leisure to write. Do not be troubled that I will not recommend you as I have all my household, your livings will certainly be assured to you. Adieu. I have no more time to write. Send to me in writing all that you are able to find in the way of prayers and exhortations the best fitted to secure my salvation. I send you my last little ring.

Immediately Mary had finished this letter she began to write her will, and almost without lifting her pen from the paper she covered two large sheets. No one was forgotten, whether present or absent, and she distributed the little that remained to her with scrupulous impartiality and rather according to the beneficiary's needs than his services. The executors she chose were the Duc de Guise, her first cousin, the Archbishop of Glasgow, her Ambassador, the Bishop of Ross, her first chaplain, and M. de Ruysseau, her Chancellor, all four being eminently proper selections for the position, the first because of his rank and influence, the bishops because of their piety and conscientiousness, and the fourth because of his knowledge of her affairs.

Her will written to her satisfaction, Mary then wrote to the King of France:

Monsieur, my brother-in-law: Having by God's will and for my sins, I believe, thrown myself into the clutches of this Queen, my cousin, and having for twenty years suffered much from weariness of spirit, I have at last been sentenced to death by her and her Parliament. Having asked for my papers, taken from me by them, in order to make my will, I have failed to recover anything useful to me, nor could I obtain permission to write down my last wishes freely, nor the promise that after my death my body should be taken as I most earnestly desire to your kingdom of which I once had the honour to be Queen, your sister and your ally. This very day, after dining, I was denounced and my sentence was told me without any pretence of respect, and like a common criminal I am to be executed tomorrow morning at eight o'clock. I have no time to relate to you fully all that has taken place; but if you deign to listen to my physician and to others of my heart-broken servants you will hear the truth that with God's help I scorn death, which I protest that I am to suffer innocent of any crime, even had I been a subject of this realm which I never was. But my adherence to the Catholic faith and my claim to the English throne are the real causes of my condemnation, and yet they will not allow me to say that I die for religion's sake, for my religion is too much for theirs. That this is true they have taken from me my chaplain and although he is imprisoned in this same castle they will not allow him to come and comfort me or to administer extreme unction, but on the other hand they have been most persistent in their endeavours to make me accept the ministrations of one of their own clergy whom they brought here for that purpose. The bearer of this letter and the rest of my servants, who are for the most part your subjects, will bear witness to the manner in which I may have performed this my last duty. And now it only remains for me to beseech you as the most Christian King, as my brother-in-law and former ally, who have often protested your friendship to me, to prove that friendship by your virtue and charity in relieving my conscience of the burden of which I cannot free it without your help, that is to say by rewarding my faithful, heart-broken servants over and above their wages; and more than that, to cause prayers to be offered for a Queen who has been called the most Christian Queen and who dies a true Catholic, bereft of all her means. So far as my son is concerned I beg you to show him such friendship as he may deserve, but my servants I commend to you unreservedly and with all my heart. I have ventured to send to you two rare stones which possess health-giving virtues, wishing that you may enjoy perfect health for many years to come; pray accept them in token of the deep affection of your dying sister-in-law.

I will recommend my servants with a letter for you, and request you, for the salvation of my soul, in whose behalf it will be expended, to order a part of your indebtedness to me to be paid, and I conjure you to do so by the honour of Jesus Christ to whom I will pray tomorrow on the scaffold that you may provide enough to endow an anniversary mass and to bestow the necessary alms.

Wednesday, two hours after midnight.

Your affectionate sister,
Marie R.

The Queen at once had copies made of these documents, including her will, and signed them all so that if the originals fell into the hands of the English the others might still reach their destinations. Bourgoin suggested that it was inadvisable to hasten to seal them as it was very possible that in the course of two or three hours she might think of something she would like to add. But the Queen declined to follow his advice, for she said that she was sure that she had forgotten nothing and that even if she had she had no time left for anything but prayer and the searching of her conscience. She then put all her belongings in the drawers of a wardrobe and handed the key to Bourgoin. A foot-bath was brought to her and she remained seated at it for about ten minutes before going to bed, but not to sleep, for her attendants saw that she was constantly repeating prayers or in rapt meditation.

Towards four in the morning, the Queen, who had for long been in the habit of having someone read to her the life of some saint or person mentioned in holy writ after her evening prayers, chose not to depart from that practice on this occasion. After some hesitation as to her choice at such a crisis in her life, she chose to have read to her the story of the repentant thief who was crucified with Christ.

"For all he was a great sinner," she said, with humility, "he was less culpable than me, and so I will pray to him in memory of the passion of Jesus Christ that pity may be had for me, even as our Blessed Lord had pity on him."

When the reading was finished she asked to have all her handkerchiefs brought to her, and selected the most beautiful among them, embroidered with gold, as a bandage for her eyes.

At dawn, having only two more hours to live, Mary rose and began to dress. But before she was fully dressed Bourgoin came in and implored her to send for all her household who were not previously present and read her will over to them, because he feared that otherwise some of them might, if they happened to be disappointed with it, accuse those who had been present of having influenced the Queen to increase their inheritances at the expense of the absentees. The Queen at once agreed to this suggestion.

She called together the whole of her household and read her will, saying that it had been made voluntarily, that it fully expressed her wishes, and that it was written throughout and signed with her own hand. She, therefore, begged them all to do everything that lay in their power to secure its execution with neither omission nor change. Then having received their promise to abide by its conditions she handed it to Bourgoin, enjoining him to give it to Monsieur de Guise, her principal executor, together with her letter to the King and other important papers. She then asked for the casket in which she had put the various purses she had filled and unfastened them one after the other. As she saw by the slip of paper which she had placed in each for whom it was intended she gave it to that person with her own hand. Not one of the recipients knew what each purse contained. The gifts varied from twenty to three hundred crowns. To these she added seven hundred pounds to be distributed among the poor—two hundred to those in England and the remainder to those in France—and to each man in personal attendance on her she gave two rose nobles to be distributed in alms at their discretion. Lastly, she gave one hundred and fifty crowns to Bourgoin to be divided among them all when they went their different ways. Thus some twenty-six or twenty-seven persons received remembrances in money.

The Queen did all these things calmly, perfectly serenely, and without the slightest change of expression—indeed, it was if she were merely preparing for a journey or a change of abode. She took leave of her servants once more, consoling them and enjoining them to live at peace with one another, and all the while she was completing her toilet and doing her best to make herself as beautiful as possible.

Her toilet completed she went from her bedroom to the ante-room where there was a covered altar at which, before she was deprived of his services, her chaplain used to celebrate mass. She knelt upon the steps, with all her household about her, and began to recite the prayers of the communion service. When she had finished she took from a gold box a wafer consecrated by Pius V which she had always carefully preserved for the time of her death; she passed it to Bourgoin and bade him perform the functions of priest as he was the oldest of her retainers, age being a venerable and holy thing. Thus, despite all the pains taken to deprive her of that consolation, Mary received the blessed sacrament of the Lord's Supper.

Upon the conclusion of this ceremony Bourgoin told the Queen that in making her will she had forgotten three persons, Mademoiselle Beauregard, Mademoiselle de Montbrun, and her chaplain. She was astonished at her unintentional forgetfulness and, taking back this document, she inserted her wishes regarding them along the border of the first page. Then she knelt again and resumed her prayers, but had almost immediately to rise as she found kneeling painful. Bourgoin sent for a little bread and wine, and she ate and drank, and when she had finished she gave him her hand and thanked him for having waited on her at her last meal. Having thus renewed her strength she knelt again to pray.

She had no more than begun when someone knocked on the door. The Queen realized what it meant, but as she had not finished her devotions she begged them who had come for her to wait a few moments, saying that she would be ready in a very short time.

The Earls of Kent and Shrewsbury, recalling her resistance when she was required to appear before the commissioners, ordered a number of guards up to the ante-room where they waited so that they might be prepared to remove her by force if she refused to go voluntarily, or if any of her servants attempted to detain her. It is not true, as some writers have stated, that the two earls insisted on entering her rooms. They entered her rooms only once, when they came to read her sentence to her.

The earls waited some minutes in accordance with the Queen's request, but just before eight o'clock there was another knock; the guards were standing behind them. To their surprise the door was immediately opened and Mary was to be seen still kneeling and praying. Thereupon, Sir Thomas Andrew, the Sheriff of Northamptonshire, entered alone bearing a white staff, and as they all remained on their knees he walked the length of the room slowly and halted behind the Queen. He stood there an instant and then said, as Mary did not seem to be aware of his presence,

"Madam, I come from their lordships."

At that the Queen at once rose to her feet, her prayer unfinished.

"Let us go," she said, and made ready to follow him.

Whereupon Bourgoin took down the ebony cross with a Christ in ivory upon it, and said to her, "Madame, do you wish to take this little crucifix with you?"

"My thanks for reminding me," Mary replied. "I intended taking it but had forgotten."

She handed it to Annibal Stewart, her valet, to be passed to her at such time as she asked for it, and walked towards the door leaning heavily on Bourgoin because of the pain in her legs. But when they were near the door he suddenly withdrew his arm and said,

"Madam, Your Majesty knows that we all love you and will gladly obey you and die for you. But I, for one, have not the strength to support you further. Nor, indeed, is it fitting that we who would defend you as long as we have a drop of blood left to shed should seem to betray you by delivering you thus into the hands of the infamous English."

"You are right, Bourgoin," the Queen answered, "and, moreover, my death would be a sad spectacle for you and one which I ought not to inflict upon your years and your affection." And turning to Sir Thomas Andrew she said, "Sir, summon someone to support me for you see that I cannot walk unaided."

The Sheriff bowed and signed to two guards whom he had placed behind the door to approach and support her, which they instantly did. She then continued on her way, preceded and followed by her household, weeping and wringing their hands. But at the second door the members of her household were stopped by other guards who said they could go no further. They cried out with one voice against such an order, saying that they had for nineteen years shared the Queen's imprisonment, had followed her from prison to prison, and that it was a frightful thing to deprive their mistress of their services in her last moments, that such an order had doubtless been issued for no other reason than to prevent their witnessing some dreadful torture which they intended to inflict upon her.

Bourgoin, who was at their head, seeing that neither threats nor entreaties were of the slightest use demanded to speak with the earls, but no attention was paid to him. When the servants tried to force a passage the guards beat them back with their arquebuses.

"That is cruel of you," the Queen said, "to forbid my servants to follow me. Like them, I begin to believe that, aside from my death, you have some evil design upon me."

"Madam," the Sheriff answered, "four of your servants are assigned to attend you, and no more. When you have descended they will be sent for and will join you."

"What!" exclaimed the Queen, "cannot even these four accompany me now?"

"Such are the earls' orders, Madam, and to my great regret I cannot depart from them."

The Queen then turned and took the crucifix from Annibal Stewart with one hand, and with the other, her Book of Hours and handkerchief.

"My children," she said, "this is one more grief added to the griefs we already have. Let us bear it like Christians and offer this new sacrifice to Almighty God."

As she spoke cries and sobs broke out on all sides. The

wretched servants fell on their knees, and while some rolled on the floor and tore at their hair, others kissed her hands and knees and the hem of her dress asking forgiveness for anything that she might have to reproach them for, calling her their mother and bidding her farewell. But the Sheriff, deeming that the scene had already lasted too long, gave a signal upon which the guards thrust them all, men and women alike, back into the room and closed the door upon them. Even through the closed door the Queen could hear their cries and lamentations which would follow her to the scaffold.

At the top of the staircase, the Queen found Andrew Melville awaiting her. He had been her Steward, long separated from her, but he had succeeded in obtaining permission to see her once more at the moment of her death. The Queen quickened her steps as she neared him and knelt to receive his blessing, which he gave her through his tears.

"Melville," she said, still kneeling, "you have been my faithful servant and friend, be the same to my son. Go to him immediately after my death and describe to him all its details. Tell him that I wish him every earthly blessing and that I pray God to send down His Holy Spirit upon him."

"Madam," Melville replied, "that is surely the saddest mission with which a man could be entrusted. But, no matter, I swear that I will faithfully carry it out."

"What do you say, Melville?" rejoined the Queen, rising. "On the contrary, what better news could you bear to him that I am at last delivered from all my suffering? Tell him that he ought to rejoice that his mother's troubles are ended. Say to him that I die a Catholic steadfast to my faith, a true Scot and Frenchwoman, and that I forgive those responsible for my death. Tell him that it has always been my wish that Scotland and England should be united, and finally, that I have done nothing which could injure his realm or prejudice his standing as a sovereign prince. And so, my good Melville, farewell until we meet again in heaven."

Leaning on the old man, whose face was wet with tears, she descended the staircase and was met at the foot by the two earls, Sir Henry Talbot, the son of the Earl of Shrewsbury, Sir Amyas Paulett, Drury, Beale, and a number of other gentlemen of the county. She walked towards them without any arrogance, but equally without humility, and complained that her household had been refused permission to accompany her. She asked that such permission be granted. The earls conferred together for a moment, after which the Earl of Kent asked whose presence she desired, and said that she might select six.

The Queen gave the names of Bourgoin, Gorjon, Gervais and Didier among the men, and Jean Kennedy and Elspeth Curle among the women, they being her particular favourites, although the last-named was the sister of the secretary who had betrayed her. But here a new difficulty arose, the earls saying that the permission did not extend to women as they were unaccustomed to such spectacles and when they were admitted to them they created a disturbance with their cries and lamentations. Moreover, as soon as the axe had fallen they darted to the scaffold to staunch the flow of blood with their handkerchiefs, all of which was highly improper.

"Gentlemen," the Queen said, "I will promise for these two women that they will do none of these things which you fear. Alas, poor creatures, they will be very comforted to bid me farewell. I trust that your mistress, a virgin and a queen, and therefore keenly alive to the honour of her sex, gave you orders that are not so strict that you are not empowered to grant me this small concession that I ask. Especially," she added in a most sorrowful voice, "as some little respect should be shown for my rank, for I am your Queen's cousin, grand-daughter of Henry VII, Queen Dowager of France, and the anointed Queen of Scotland."

The earls again consulted together and ended by granting her request. Two guards went upstairs at once to fetch the persons named.

Mary went on towards the great hall, supported by the two gentlemen called upon to do so by Sir Amyas Paulett, accompanied and followed by the earls and the others, the Sheriff leading the procession, and Andrew Melville carrying her train. Her toilet, upon which she had bestowed all the care that she had it in her power to do, consisted of a head-dress of fine cambric edged with lace, with a lace veil thrown back over her shoulder and touching the ground. Her dress was of black brocaded satin lined with black taffeta and trimmed in front with sable with a long train and flowing sleeves which hung almost to the floor; the buttons were of jet in the shape of acorns and edged with pearls; the collar was cut *à l'Italienne*; she wore a doublet of black-figured satin and over it a bodice of crimson satin, laced behind, and trimmed with crimson velvet. Around her neck was a string of scented beads from which hung a gold cross, and two rosaries hung from her girdle. It was thus dressed that she entered the great hall where the scaffold was erected.

It was a wooden platform some two feet high and twelve feet square, surrounded by a railing and covered with black serge. Upon it was a low stool, a cushion for her to kneel on, and the block, which was similarly covered with a black cloth.

After ascending the two steps, and as she stepped on to the fatal boards, the executioner came towards her and knelt upon one knee to ask her forgiveness for what he was about to do. Although he held his axe behind him as he did so, he did not succeed in hiding it from Mary who cried out when she saw it,

"Ah, I would far rather be beheaded with a sword as is done in France!"

"It is not my fault, Madam," the man replied, "that this last wish of Your Majesty's cannot be gratified, for I was not ordered to bring a sword, and finding nothing but this axe I must of necessity use it. Will that stop you from forgiving me?"

"I forgive you freely, my friend," Mary said, "and see, in proof of this, I give you my hand to kiss."

Having touched the Queen's hand with his lips the man rose and brought forward the stool, and Mary seated herself. The Earls of Kent and Shrewsbury stood at her left, the Sheriff and the executioner in front of her, Sir Amyas Paulett behind, and, outside the railing, lords, knights and gentlemen to the number of about two hundred and fifty. Beale then began to read for the second time the decree of condemnation. While he was reading the opening words those of the Queen's household who had been sent for entered the hall and took their places behind the scaffold: the men stood on a bench against the wall and the two women knelt in front of the bench. At the same moment the Queen's little spaniel, of which she was very fond, slipped noiselessly into the hall as if he feared to be driven away and lay down beside his mistress.

The Queen listened without appearing to pay any great attention, as if it did not concern her. Her expression throughout was as tranquil, indeed as joyous, as if it were a pardon and not a death warrant. When Beale had finished and called out "God Save Queen Elizabeth!", without evoking any response, Mary crossed herself and stood erect with no change of expression; she seemed lovelier than ever.

"My lords," she said, "I was born a queen, a sovereign princess not subject to the laws, closely related to the Queen of England, and her lawful successor. I have for long been a prisoner in this country. I have endured great suffering and humiliation which no one had the right to inflict upon me, and now, to crown it all, I am to lose my life. I call all here to witness that I die in the Catholic faith, thankful that God has allowed me to die in his sacred cause, and protesting today as always, in public and in private, that I have never conspired to bring about, consented to, or desired the death of the Queen of England, nor any injury whatever to her person. But that, on the contrary, I have always loved her, and have always offered her good and reasonable conditions for the settlement of the discords in her kingdom and my deliverance from captivity. All this I have done, my lords, as you well know, without ever having been honoured with a reply from her. My enemies have at last achieved their purpose, which was to accomplish my death. Nevertheless, I forgive them as I forgive all those who have plotted against me or wished me ill. After my death the authors will be known who contrived it and persisted in bringing it about. But I die with no accusation on my lips, lest the Lord hear and avenge me."

Then, whether because he feared that such a speech by so exalted a woman would have too great an effect on the assembly, or because so many words caused too great delay, the Dean of Peterborough stood in front of Mary, resting himself against the railing.

"Madam, my most honoured mistress commanded me to come to you . . ."

He got no further than this when Mary broke in upon him.

"Sir," she said firmly, "I have no need of you. I do not wish to hear you and I beg that you will desist."

"Madam," persisted the Dean in the face of her firm and clearly expressed determination, "you have but a few moments more to live. Change your opinions, abjure your false doctrines, and rest your faith on Jesus Christ alone that through him you may be saved."

"All that you can say is of no avail," the Queen replied, "and you will gain nothing by it. I therefore beg that you be silent and let me die in peace."

As she saw that he wished to continue she sat down on the other side of the stool with her back to him. But the Dean immediately made a circuit of the scaffold and once more faced her. But when he opened his mouth to speak the Queen turned back to her original position. Watching this the Earl of Shrewsbury said,

"Madam, I am in despair that you are so wedded to the

follies of popery. Permit us, I beg you, to let us pray for you."

"If you choose to pray for me, my lord, I am grateful, for your intention is kind. But I cannot join you in your prayers for we are not of the same religion."

The Earl then called to the Dean and, while the Queen upon her stool was praying in an undertone, he knelt upon the steps of the scaffold and prayed in a loud voice. His words were repeated after him by the whole assembly except Mary and her attendants. In the middle of her prayers, which she was repeating with the gold cross on her necklace of beads, her crucifix in one hand and in the other her Book of Hours, she suddenly slid to her knees, praying aloud in Latin while the others prayed in English. When they paused she began in English so that they might understand her prayers—for the afflicted Church of Christ, for an end to the persecution of Catholics, and for God's blessing on the reign of her son, fervently declaring that she hoped to be saved by the merits of Jesus Christ at the foot of whose cross she was about to pour out her blood.

At these words the Earl of Kent could contain himself no longer, and regardless of the solemnity of the moment cried out.

"God's wounds, Madam, take Jesus Christ into your heart and cast out such papish rubbish!"

But she went on, not heeding him, imploring the saints to intercede with God on her behalf, and kissing her crucifix she cried,

"Lord! Lord! Take me into Thine arms outstretched upon the cross and forgive all my sins."

She again took her seat upon the stool. The Earl of Kent asked her if she had no frank confession to make, to which she replied that as she had committed no crime any confession she might make would be lies.

"Very well, Madam," the earl replied, "if that be so, prepare to die."

The Queen rose and said to the executioner who had

approached to uncover her head and neck, "Let me do it, my friend, for I know better than you how it should be done and I am not accustomed to being uncovered before so large a company, nor by such an attendant."

She then called to her two women and began to remove the pins from her headdress. As Jean Kennedy and Elspeth Curle helped their mistress for the last time they could not hold back their tears.

"Do not weep," Mary said in French, "for I gave my word that you would not."

As she spoke she made the sign of the cross on the forehead of each, kissed them both, and asked them to pray for her. The Queen then began to undress, helping her attendants as she was in the habit of doing when retiring for the night. She took the gold cross from her neck and was about to give it to Jean Kennedy, saying to the executioner,

"My friend, I know that everything I have upon me belongs to you, but you have no use for this so let me give it to the young lady, I beg, and she will pay you double its value in money."

But the executioner scarcely allowed her to finish the sentence before he snatched it from her saying, "It's my entitlement."

The Queen showed no emotion at his brutality, but continued to take off her clothing until she stood only in her petticoat. She then sat down again upon the stool. Jean Kennedy took from her pocket the cambric handkerchief Mary had chosen the previous night and bandaged her eyes with it to the great astonishment of the earls and others as this was not customary in England.

Supposing that she was to be beheaded in the French manner, that is as she sat upon the stool, Mary sat perfectly erect with stiffened neck to make the executioner's task the easier. He, uncertain how to act, stood with his axe in his hand, but did not strike. At last his assistant laid hold of the Queen's head and drew her forward until she fell upon her knees.

Mary seemed then to realize what was expected of her and groped round for the block still holding in her hands her Book of Hours and the crucifix. Finding it she laid her neck upon it and placed her clasped hands under her chin to be able to pray until the last moment. But the assistant drew her hands away lest they be cut off with her head.

As Mary exclaimed, "*In manus tuas, Domine*" the executioner raised his axe, which was one of the ordinary wood-cutting sort, and struck. But he struck too high and the blade entered the skull, causing the book and the crucifix to fall from the sufferer's hands, but not detaching the head. Stunned by the blow the Queen did not move and thus the executioner could prepare for the second stroke at his leisure. But even then the head did not fall and a third stroke was needed to sever the shred of flesh which still held it to the shoulders. At last it fell and the executioner held it up for all to see, saying "God Save Queen Elizabeth."

"So may perish all Her Majesty's enemies," the Dean of Peterborough intoned.

"Amen," said the Earl of Kent—but he was the only one, for every other voice was choked by tears and sobs.

Chapter 13

It was then that Mary's wig became unfastened. They could see her hair, cut very short, and as white as that of a woman of seventy. Her face had changed so much during this past agony that it had become unrecognizable. The sight of it evoked exclamations of horror, for the eyes were open and the lips moved as if she still prayed. This nervous movement lasted for more than a quarter of an hour after her head had been severed from her body.

The members of her household present at her execution rushed on to the scaffold and gathered up her Book of Hours and crucifix as priceless relics.

Jean Kennedy remembered the little dog and sought for him everywhere, calling him by name, but he had disappeared. A little later, as the executioner was untying the Queen's garters, which were of blue satin embroidered with silver, he saw the poor little creature hiding under the petticoat from where he had to be forcibly removed. But the animal escaped from his grasp and took refuge between his dead mistress's shoulders and her head, which had been deposited by the body. Jean Kennedy picked him up, not heeding his piteous howls, and carried him away all covered as he was with blood, for the order had been given for everyone to leave the hall. Bourgoin and Gervais stayed behind to beg Sir Amyas Paulett to allow them to remove the Queen's heart so that they could take it to France as they had promised her. Their request was roughly refused and they were pushed out of the hall. All the doors were then closed, leaving the executioner with the corpse.

Brantôme relates that an infamous thing then happened. Two hours after the execution the body and the head were taken to the room in which Mary Stuart had appeared before the commissioners and placed upon the table where the judges had sat. The remains were covered with a black serge cloth and lay there until three in the afternoon when Walters, a physician fron Standford, with a surgeon of the village of Fotheringay, came to open and embalm the body. This they did in the presence of Paulett and the soldiers, without the slightest consideration for the rank and sex of the hapless creature whose body was thus exposed to the gaze of those who wished to watch. This indignity did not, however, serve its purpose. For although it was rumoured that the Queen's legs were swollen from dropsy, those present were forced to admit that they had never seen a girl's body in the flower of her youth more spotless and beautiful than Mary Stuart's. This was in spite of her violent death after nineteen years of suffering and captivity.

When the body was opened the spleen was found to be healthy, the veins a little pale, the lungs yellowish in spots. Everything promised a long life to her whose days had been so cruelly cut short. After a formal report had been written the body was embalmed and put into a leaden coffin which was then placed in another of wood. It was left lying on the table until the first of August, nearly five months after the execution. During that time no one was allowed to go near it. When it was discovered that Mary's unfortunate servants, who were still held prisoner, were in the habit of gazing through the keyhole at the coffin which contained all that remained of their beloved mistress the keyhole was blocked so that even that scant comfort was denied them.

Within an hour of Mary Stuart's death Sir Henry Talbot rode off at full speed for London to carry to Elizabeth the news of her rival's death. True to her character, Elizabeth on reading the first lines of the message displayed the utmost grief and indignation; she said that her orders had been misunderstood, that there had been too much haste, and that it was all the fault of Davison, the secretary, to whom she had given the warrant to be retained and not to be sent to Fotheringay until she could finally make up her mind. As a result Davison was sent to the Tower and sentenced to a fine of ten thousand pounds for having failed to obey the Queen's orders.

However, in the midst of her show of grief, Elizabeth put an embargo on all vessels in the various ports of England so that the news of the Queen of Scotland's death might not be carried to foreign countries, especially to France, except by diplomatic emissaries who could make it appear in a more favourable light in so far as Elizabeth was concerned. At the same time the scandalous popular rejoicings which greeted the news of Mary's arrest were repeated in celebration of the news of her execution. Bonfires were lighted in the streets. Enthusiasm was such that the French Embassy was broken into and the furniture taken to feed the fires when they began to die down.

M. de Chateauneuf, not yet recovered from the outrage, was still barricaded in his Embassy when he received an invitation from Elizabeth a fortnight after the execution to visit her at the Archbishop of Canterbury's country house. He went, determined to keep silent about what had taken place, but as soon as he arrived, Elizabeth, dressed in black, went to meet him. She overwhelmed him with kindness and told him that she was prepared to place all her available forces at the disposal of Henri III to assist him in crushing the League. De Chateauneuf received all her offers with a cold, stern expression, persevering in his intention of saying nothing about the event which had caused them both to wear mourning. But Elizabeth took his hand, drew him aside, and said with a heavy sigh, "Ah, Monsieur, since I last saw you a great misfortune has befallen me. I speak of the death of my good sister the Queen of Scotland, of which I swear by God himself and my soul's salvation that I am absolutely innocent. I signed the warrant, it is true, but some of my council tricked me, which I cannot forgive. And I swear to God that were it not for the long years they have been in my service I would execute them. I have a woman's body, Monsieur, but in that woman's body is a man's heart."

De Chateauneuf bowed without replying. But his letter to Henri III and the latter's reply prove that neither of them was for one single instant duped by this female Tiberius.

Meanwhile, as is known, Mary Stuart's unfortunate servants remained in captivity at Fotheringay and the disfigured body lay there awaiting royal burial. Elizabeth claimed that this state of affairs existed because she needed time to arrange for the spectacular funeral she intended giving "her good sister Mary". The real reason was that she did not dare have the public, royal burial so close upon the secret, infamous death. Furthermore, it was essential that such reports as it pleased Elizabeth to circulate should have time to gain credence before the real truth should become known from the lips of Mary's household. The Queen hoped that when the world had once formed an opinion regarding Mary Stuart's death it would be too indifferent to change it. So it was not until the gaolers were as weary as the prisoners that Elizabeth, having been officially informed that the poorly embalmed body could be kept no longer, at last issued orders that the funeral should take place.

On 1 August 1587, tailors and dressmakers sent by Elizabeth arrived at Fotheringay with black cloth and black silk to provide all of the dead Queen's household with mourning. But this material was refused, for, not anticipating such generosity on the part of the Queen of England, they had provided their own mourning at their own expense immediately on their mistress's death. Nonetheless the tailors and dressmakers set to work and to such good purpose that everything was completed by the seventh of the month.

At about eight o'clock on the following evening a large vehicle covered with black velvet and drawn by four horses with sable trappings appeared before the gates of Fotheringay Castle. The vehicle was adorned with small banners on which were embroidered the arms of Scotland, which were the Queen's, and the arms of Aragon, which were Darnley's. It was followed by the King-at-Arms and twenty mounted gentlemen, with their retainers and lackeys, all dressed in black. The King-at-Arms dismounted and went with his suite to the hall where the body lay. The coffin was carried down and placed on the hearse with every respect, the entire party being bareheaded and preserving absolute silence.

All of this caused great excitement among the prisoners. They at once discussed the propriety of requesting permission to watch over the body of their mistress, for they could not bear the thought of it being taken away without them beside it. Just as they were on the point of sending to ask for an interview with the King-at-Arms, that dignitary entered the room where they were assembled. He told them that he had been instructed by his royal mistress to do honour to the late Queen of Scotland with the most magnificent funeral within his power to arrange, and that he was most anxious to show himself worthy of so important a mission. He had already completed most of the arrangements for the ceremony to take place on the tenth of the month, in two days time, and that as the leaden casket containing the corpse was very heavy, it was thought best to take it that night to the place where the grave had been prepared rather than to wait until the day fixed for the burial. They, therefore, had no occasion for alarm as this removal of the casket was merely a preliminary ceremony. He went on to say that if any of them wished to accompany the body and to see the arrangements that were being made, they were free to do so, and the others could follow later, for it was Queen Elizabeth's explicit command that all of them, from the highest to the lowest, should be present at the funeral ceremonies.

This assurance eased the minds of the unhappy prisoners

who authorized Bourgoin, Gervais, and six others to be chosen by them, to follow the body. These were Andrew Melville, Stewart, Gorjon, Howard, Lauder, and Nicolas Delamarre.

The procession left Fotheringay at ten o'clock, preceded by the King-at-Arms accompanied by men on foot carrying torches, and followed by the twenty gentlemen and their retainers. At two in the morning they arrived at Peterborough, with its magnificent cathedral built by one of the old Anglo-Saxon kings. Catherine of Aragon was buried there, on the left side of the choir; her tomb was still adorned with a canopy carrying her crest.

They found the cathedral draped in black and a structure erected in the centre of the choir after the manner of the *chapelles ardentes* in France, except that it was not surrounded by lighted candles. It was covered with black velvet embroidered with the arms of Scotland and Aragon, similar to the banners on the hearse. A resting place for the pall had been prepared beneath it; it was a bier, again covered with black velvet, fringed with silver, and upon it, on a pillow covered with similar material, there rested a crown.

To the right of the bier and facing Catherine of Aragon's sepulchre a grave had been prepared for Mary of Scotland. It was of brick and so constructed that it could be covered later with a marble slab, or a monument. The Bishop of Peterborough in his episcopal robes, without mitre, cross or cope, and accompanied by the Dean and minor clergy, awaited the arrival of the procession at the Cathedral door. The body was borne into the church without music or prayer and lowered into the grave in utter silence.

As soon as the coffin was in place the masons filled in the grave almost to the level of the surrounding pavement. An aperture a foot and a half long was left open. Through this, the contents of the grave could be seen and it would later allow, as was then customary at the obsequies of royal personages, the broken staves of office and the insignia and banners bearing the arms of the deceased to be thrown in upon the coffin.

When this nocturnal ceremony had ended, Melville, Bourgoin, and the others were conducted to the Bishop's palace where all those appointed to attend the final obsequies were to assemble. More than three hundred and fifty persons, all of whom—with the exception of the members of Mary's household—had been selected from officers of State, as well as the Protestant nobility and gentry, were present.

On the Thursday previous, the hall of the palace had been hung with splendid draperies. This had been done not so much to provide Melville, Bourgoin, and the others the satisfaction of witnessing the interment of Queen Mary, but to make them witnesses of the munificence of Queen Elizabeth. As can readily be imagined the luckless prisoners showed little warmth for this ostentatious display.

On the next day all those deputed to attend, having assembled at the palace, formed into procession in order of rank and proceeded to the nearby Cathedral. When they arrived they took the positions assigned to them in the choir. The choristers at once began to intone the funeral service in English in accordance with the Protestant ritual. At the first words of the service, when Bourgoin saw that it was not being performed by Catholic priests, he walked out, declaring that he would not assist in such a sacrilege. Bourgoin was followed by the members of Mary's household. Only Melville and Mowbray remained, reasoning that in whatever tongue prayers were offered they were heard by the Lord. The exodus caused great scandal but did not prevent the Bishop from preaching his sermon.

When the sermon was ended the King-at-Arms sought out Bourgoin and his companions, who were walking in the cloisters, told them that Holy Communion was about to be celebrated and invited them to take part in it. But they replied that as they were Catholics they could not partake of the sacrament at an unconsecrated altar. The King-at-

Arms returned, much annoyed that the ceremony should be marred by their bigotry, and the sacrament was administered. He then made a last attempt and sent word to them that the religious services were ended and that, consequently, they could return and be present at the royal ceremonies which had no connexion with any form of worship. They agreed, but by the time they had arrived the staves of office had already been broken and with the banners, thrown through the opening which the workmen were already closing up.

Then in the same order in which it had come, the procession returned to the Bishop's palace, where a sumptuous funeral banquet was spread. By a strange quirk, Elizabeth, having punished the living like a criminal, heaped royal honours upon the dead and desired that Mary's faithful household, whom she had forgotten for so long, should be the guests of honour at this feast. But they did not appreciate this rather tardy kindness, and showed neither amazement nor gratification for the banquet's magnificence. Tears choked them and they made no reply to the questions asked them and the attention lavished on them.

Immediately the meal was over, they left Peterborough and returned to Fotheringay. There they learned that they were free to go where they chose. They did not need to be told twice, for they were living in constant fear and considered their lives in danger for as long as they remained in England. They hastily collected their belongings and left Fotheringay Castle on foot on Monday, 13 August 1587.

Bourgoin was the last to leave. When he reached the further side of the drawbridge he turned around. Christian though he was, he could not forgive Elizabeth, not on account of his own sufferings but for what she had inflicted on his mistress. So it was thus that he turned about and shook his clenched fists at the regicide walls, calling out in a loud and threatening voice these words of David:

"O Lord God, give them according to their deeds, and according to the wickedness of their endeavours; give them according to the work of their hands, render to them their deserts."

The old man's curse was heard and impartial history has condemned Elizabeth.

Afterword

It has been stated that the executioner's axe, when it embedded itself in Mary Stuart's skull, caused the crucifix and Book of Hours to fall from her hands, and that they were picked up later by some person or persons of her suite. It is not known what became of the crucifix, but the Book of Hours is in the Bibliothèque Nationale in Paris where it may be seen by those who are interested in historic souvenirs. Its authenticity is vouched for by the following two certificates which are inscribed on the fly-leaf of the volume.

The first certificate:
We, the undersigned, "supérieur vicaire de l'étroite observance" of the Order of Cluny, certify that this book was delivered to us by order of the late Dom Michel Nardin, a professed priest of our Order who died at our College of Saint Martial of Avignon, on 28 March 1723, aged about eighty years, thirty of which he passed among us leading a life of exemplary piety; he was a German by birth, and served a long time as an officer in the army.

He was admitted to Cluny and took orders there, having put away all thoughts of worldly possession and honours. He retained, with the permission of his superiors, this book only, which he knew to have been in constant use by Mary Stuart, Queen of England and Scotland, to the end of her life. Before his death separated him from his brethren, he asked that the book, in order that it might more surely reach us, be sent to us in a sealed package.

In the same condition as we have received it, we have requested M. l'Abbé Bignon, Counsellor of State and Librarian to the King, to accept this precious souvenir of the piety of a Queen of England and a German officer of her faith and ours.

Signed, Frère Gérard Poncet
Supérieur vicaire-général

The second certificate:
We, Jean-Paul Bignon, Librarian to the King, are most glad to have this opportunity to demonstrate our zeal by placing this manuscript [sic] in His Majesty's library.

Signed, Jean-Pierre [sic] Bignon
8 July 1724

This book, upon which the last glance of the Queen of Scotland rested, is a duodecimo written in Gothic characters and containing prayers in Latin. It is ornamented with gold miniatures in relief representing devotional subjects, scenes from sacred history, and the lives of saints and martyrs. Each page has a border of arabesques mingled with garlands of flowers and fruits, from which grotesque faces of men and animals peer out.

The black velvet binding, now much worn, is decorated with an enamelled pansy entangled in a catkin of silver and tasselled, knotted, silver-gilt cords.